THE
WISDOM
OF THE
BULLFROG

Also by Admiral William H. McRaven

The Hero Code: Lessons Learned from Lives Well Lived
Sea Stories: My Life in Special Operations
Make Your Bed: Little Things That Can Change Your
Life...and Maybe the World

ADMIRAL
WILLIAM H. McRAVEN
(U.S. Navy Retired)

THE
WISDOM
OF THE
BULLFROG

LEADERSHIP MADE SIMPLE
(BUT NOT EASY)

**GRAND
CENTRAL**

New York Boston

Grand Central Publishing
Hachette Book Group
1290 Avenue of the Americas, New York, NY 10104
grandcentralpublishing.com
twitter.com/grandcentralpub

First Edition: April 2023

Grand Central Publishing is a division of Hachette Book Group, Inc. The Grand Central Publishing name and logo is a trademark of Hachette Book Group, Inc.

The publisher is not responsible for websites (or their content) that are not owned by the publisher.

The Hachette Speakers Bureau provides a wide range of authors for speaking events. To find out more, go to www.hachettespeakersbureau.com or email HachetteSpeakers@hbgusa.com.

Grand Central Publishing books may be purchased in bulk for business, educational, or promotional use. For information, please contact your local bookseller or the Hachette Book Group Special Markets Department at special.markets@hbgusa.com.

Library of Congress Cataloging-in-Publication Data is available.

ISBNs: 9781538707944 (hardcover), 9781538707951 (ebook), 9781538710241 (large print), 9781538742044 (signed hardcover), 9781538742037 (signed hardcover)

Printed in the United States of America

LSC

Printing 1, 2023

This book is dedicated to my wife, Georgeann, who has led me through the challenging times in my life and followed me on every adventure. I love you!

CONTENTS

INTRODUCTION

Standing at the entrance to the Basic Underwater Demolition/SEAL (BUD/S) training facility is a six-foot-tall, half-man, half-fish, reptilian monster with bulging black eyes and webbed hands and feet. His gills flaring outward and a long three-pronged trident in one hand, he has a sign around his neck that says SO YOU WANT TO BE A FROG-MAN! This Creature from the Black Lagoon challenges every student who walks across the quarterdeck and onto the asphalt Grinder—the Grinder, where for the next six months you will endure hundreds of hours of calisthenics, endless harassment by battle-hardened warriors, and physical and mental pain the likes of which you have never encountered. Add to this challenge hours of bone-chilling ocean swims, miles and miles of soft-sand runs, brutal obstacle courses, and the all-consuming Hell Week.

Thirty-four years after I started BUD/S training, I would

be anointed as the Bull Frog[*]—the longest-serving frogman and Navy SEAL on active duty. In almost four decades of service, I learned a lot about what it took to be a frogman and to lead frogmen. But I was also honored to lead countless others: Green Berets, Rangers, Air Force pilots, and Special Tactics operators; Marine Raiders, infantrymen, ship and submarine officers, intelligence and law enforcement professionals, civil servants, doctors, researchers, technicians, students and faculty. From midshipman to four-star admiral to chancellor of the University of Texas System, each day, each week, each month, each year, each decade would bring new leadership lessons. Some lessons came easy, others brought great pain, but all lessons were of value. All lessons would serve me well in dealing with the challenges that life presented.

But leadership, no matter whether you are a midshipman or an admiral, is never easy. Even those who seem to carry the burden of leadership with ease often struggle. Carl von Clausewitz, the great nineteenth-century general who wrote the consummate book *On War*, once said that "everything in war is simple, but the simple things

---

[*] For the first year, I shared the award with my good friend Commander Brian Sebenaler, until his retirement in 2012.

are difficult." In 2009, on a return trip to Afghanistan, I was reading a foreign policy magazine. There were two articles in the magazine written by a couple of East Coast academics. The professors explained how the U.S. military just didn't understand the best way to win the war in Afghanistan. They wrote, rather condescendingly, that if the military would only build roads, they could connect the villages to the districts. Then with more roads they could connect the districts to the provinces and finally the provinces to the capital. Building all these roads would allow the Afghans to prosper and be strong enough to defeat the Taliban. *All the military had to do was build roads.* Well, no kidding! Why didn't we think of that? Well, we did think of that! It's just that when people are shooting at you and trying to blow you up—it's hard to build roads. And that, dear reader, is the nature of leadership as well. Everything in leadership is simple, it's just that the simplest things are difficult. It would be simple to say, "Be men and women of great integrity" or "Lead from the front" or "Take care of your troops," but it is difficult to do. Why? Because we are humans and each of us has our foibles, our weaknesses, and our shortfalls that can affect how we lead. *But as difficult as leadership is, it is not complicated.*

In its simplest form, leadership is "accomplishing a task

with the people and resources you have while maintaining the integrity of your institution." A good leader knows both how to inspire the men and women that work for them and how to manage the people and resources necessary to complete the task. But leadership is not *just* about getting the job done. It is also about maintaining or advancing the reputation of your institution. How many times have we read about a university athletic program that was excelling in athletics but was caught in a cheating scandal along the way? Or a financial institution that made its stockholders a lot of money but eventually collapsed because they violated the law? If as a leader you fail the institution you are leading, then you have failed—period. Once again, leadership is difficult, but not complicated. To do it right doesn't require a sophisticated chart, a calculus formula, or a complex algorithm, but it does require some guidance.

So, how do we make the difficult nature of leadership simple? Well, for thousands of years militaries have relied on mottoes, creeds, parables, and stories to inspire, to motivate, and to guide leaders and followers alike. These sayings serve to reinforce certain behaviors. They also provide a memory prompt, a Pavlovian response, and an inspirational surge that helps direct individual actions in the midst of uncertainty.

Serving in the military, I relied heavily on these sayings to guide my actions. Whenever I had a difficult decision to make, I would ask myself, *"Can you stand before the long green table?"* Since WWII, the conference tables used in military boardrooms had been constructed of long, narrow pieces of furniture covered in green felt. Whenever a formal proceeding took place that required multiple officers to adjudicate an issue, the officers would gather around the table. The point of the saying was simple. If you *couldn't* make a good case to the officers sitting around the long green table, then you should reconsider your actions. Every time I was about to make an important decision, I asked myself, "Can I stand before the long green table and be satisfied that I took all the right actions?" It is one of the most fundamental questions a leader must ask themselves—and the old saying helped me remember what steps to take.

But there are other mottoes and sayings that have equal power. The Army Rangers' *Sua Sponte* (Of Your Own Accord); the British Special Air Service motto, *Who Dares Wins*; and the SEAL mantra, *The Only Easy Day Was Yesterday*; all these sayings have a storied history that drove leaders at the time to make certain profound decisions. They inspired action in the heat of battle and served to strengthen the leader's resolve and to motivate the troops.

These sayings are not just words, they are words born of experience, trial by fire, and most written in blood. Words worth remembering as we try to shape our response to a problem.

In this book I have collected eighteen of these sayings that have guided me throughout my career: mottoes, parables, creeds, and stories that have served me well when I was starting a new assignment or had a particularly difficult leadership challenge.

The eighteen chapters are a mix of Personal Qualities and Professional Actions. Every leader must have certain qualities that they exhibit in their personal life if they hope to lead well. But a strong character alone is not sufficient for success. As a leader you must take actions to build a plan, communicate its intent, inspect its progress, hold people (and yourself) accountable. Together, qualities and actions are the building blocks of great leaders.

The road to becoming the Bull Frog was not easy. No road to the top ever is, but I hope you will find wisdom in these pages that will make your road to the top much easier to travel.

CHAPTER ONE

Death Before Dishonor

The most tragic thing in the world is a man of genius who is not a man of honor.

—GEORGE BERNARD SHAW

onor. It sounds a bit quaint in today's vernacular. A gentleman's honor. A lady's honor. To honor thy mother and father. The Honorable Judge so-and-so. But for thousands of years, honor has had meaning. It has had value. It was—and still is—considered paramount to who you are. Do you honor your family by being a man or woman of virtue? Do you honor your country by serving in times of need? Do you honor your faith by being pious and reverent?

Legend has it that the phrase "Death Before Dishonor" began with the Greek Stoics who were prepared to die rather than compromise their values. Later, Julius Caesar is quoted as saying "I love the name of honor more than I fear death." The samurai of Japan were steeped in the tradition of honor and always prepared to die rather than dishonor their service to the emperor. And in modern times, the United States Marine Corps has unofficially adopted the saying "Death Before Dishonor" after legendary Marine sergeant John Basilone had the motto tattooed on his left arm.

Unfortunately, over the millennia there have been men and women who cloaked themselves in "honor" only to be as unscrupulous and as vile as any humans in history. But true honor—doing the right thing for the right reasons—is the foundation of great leadership. With it, your colleagues will follow you through the trials and hardships of your quest. But without honor, nothing you accomplish will be of lasting value. And if you dishonor your company, your family, your country, or your faith, then your legacy of leadership will forever be tainted.

———

As I approached the podium in the Great Hall of the United States Military Academy, I couldn't help but be impressed by the cadets standing before me. Immaculately attired in their gray mess dress uniform, replete with brass buttons and gold stripes, here were America's finest: young men and women who had volunteered to join the Army during a time of war, knowing that by raising their hands they were likely to find themselves in conflict during their years of service.

Around the room were reminders of the remarkable soldiers that had gone before them: Grant, Pershing,

Eisenhower, Patton, and MacArthur. The symbols of America's commitment to the values of Duty, Honor, and Country hung from the walls.

It was 2014, and as the commander of the United States Special Operations Command, I had been invited to be the guest speaker at the 500th Night event, a gala that marked the last five hundred days before the West Point juniors graduated. Being neither an academy graduate nor an Army officer, I was quite honored to have the opportunity to address them. I entitled my remarks "A Sailor's Perspective on the Army." Having spent the past twelve years of war serving alongside some remarkable soldiers, I thought I could provide a little perspective to the young cadets. A perspective not colored by my service uniform.

I began by making it clear that the Army they were joining was not the Army of the Hudson, the Army of the history books, or the Army portrayed on the countless murals across campus. This was today's Army, with today's problems, with today's soldiers, soldiers who were in need of real leadership. Leadership sounds simple in the books, I offered, but it is quite difficult in real life. Leadership is difficult because it is a human interaction, and nothing is more daunting, more frustrating, more complex than trying to lead men and women in tough times. Those officers who do it well earn respect because, unfortunately, doing it poorly is commonplace.

I had chosen those last words carefully because earlier in the day I had passed by the Cadet Honor Code, which is etched in glass set in a stone wall that adorns the academy grounds. The code is simple but incredibly powerful. It says:

"A cadet will not lie, cheat, steal, or tolerate those who do."

Below the Honor Code is the mission of the United States Military Academy. The mission of West Point is not to produce Pattonesque geniuses, four-star generals, or presidents of the United States. The mission is to produce "leaders of character." And the Honor Code provides the foundation of that character. The code beckons young men and women who aspire "to live above the common level of life."

To live above the common level of life: to be noble when others may be unprincipled, to be honorable when others may be shameless, to be men and women of integrity when others may resort to dishonesty. What I found in leading and being led by great officers from all branches of service was the importance of character and having a personal code of honor to help guide you through the difficult times.

It is easy when we see generals fall, when their foibles are made public and their failures of character are laid bare, to believe that that code is nothing but hollow words to inspire impressionable young men and women. It is easy to get jaded by the ugliness of life and to become cynical when those we held up as heroes stumble. But make no mistake about it, if you want to be a great leader you must have a personal code of conduct that provides an anchor for your decisions and your actions. An anchor that tethers you to a good place of return when you go astray. And most of us will go astray at some point. We are all human. We make poor decisions. We act stupidly. We have regrets. But nevertheless, we should all strive—and strive mightily—to be honorable.

When I joined the SEAL Teams in 1978, all the operators were Vietnam vets. They were tough, salty, irreverent, and at times insubordinate, but there was still a sense of nobility to them that shaped their character. Even though they had endured a difficult, nasty war that at times tested their humanity, they understood the need to be men of integrity, men of honor.

And, like their Vietnam forebears, today's SEALs are not without their dark shadows, but the *standard* of conduct

7

is still exceptionally high. In 2005, the modern SEALs codified that standard of conduct in the Navy SEAL Ethos, which reads in part:

I serve with honor on and off the battlefield... Uncompromising integrity is my standard...My word is my bond.

The SEAL Ethos mirrors the code of conduct of so many other military units. The Army Ranger Creed says, "I will always endeavor to uphold the prestige, honor, and high esprit de corps of my Ranger Regiment." Similarly, the Green Berets' creed says "I pledge to uphold the honor and integrity [of the Green Beret] legacy in all that I am— in all that I do." Marine Raiders: "I will uphold the honor of the legacy and valor passed down to me. I will do the right thing always...I will not bring shame upon myself or those with whom I serve."

But of course, it's not just the military. The Girl Scout Law says, "I will do my best to be honest and fair...[and] make the world a better place." The Boy Scouts' oath says, "On my honor I will do my best...and [be] morally straight." And I believe the original Hippocratic Oath captures the importance of a creed better than any other.

The final paragraph of the Hippocratic Oath says, "So long as I maintain this Oath faithfully and without corruption, may it be granted to me to partake of life fully…gaining the respect of all men for all time. However, should I transgress this Oath and violate it, may the opposite be my fate."

There are always examples of successful people who lack scruples, who have no moral compass yet have made billions of dollars and driven their industries to new heights. But more often than not, that lack of integrity, doing wrong instead of right, can manifest itself in a toxic work culture, a failed business, or a personal tragedy.

If you violate your oath, your code of conduct, the basic decency with which you should live your life and run your business, then eventually you will lose the respect of the men and women you serve, and *the opposite becomes your fate*.

Doing what is right matters because, when exhibited by a leader on a daily basis, it develops the culture of the institution, and it develops the next generation of leaders. If you are a person who lacks character, then the culture of the organization will reflect that, and you will be setting up the next generation of leaders for failure.

I often hear that it's hard to know the right thing to do. *No, it's not!* You always know what's right, but sometimes it's just very hard to do it. It's hard because you may have to admit failure. It's hard because the right decision may affect your friends and colleagues. It's hard because you may not personally benefit from doing what's right. Yeah, it's hard. That's called leadership.

Having a set of moral principles and being a person of integrity are the most important virtues for any leader. In the simplest terms it follows the West Point Honor Code: Don't lie, cheat, steal, or tolerate those that do. This means be honest with your workforce, your customers, and the public. Be fair in your business dealings. Follow the Golden Rule: Treat others as you would have others treat you. If this sounds a bit Pollyannaish or like you're in Sunday school, so be it. Being a person of high integrity is what separates the great leaders from the commonplace.

After thirty-seven years as a Navy SEAL, I am too mindful of my own shortfalls to be overly self-righteous in telling the reader how to behave. However, in spite of my many stumbles along the way, I always found that having a set of principles helped me during the most challenging times of my life and my career.

Before you can master any of the other axioms of wisdom, you must first strive to be men and women of honor and integrity. That is what sets the great leaders above the commonplace. It will not be easy. It never is. But it is also not complicated.

It's Simple:

1. Be fair and honorable in your business dealings. It's the only way that you and your employees can leave a legacy to be proud of.
2. Never lie, cheat, steal, or tolerate those who do. The culture of your organization starts with you.
3. Own your lapses in judgment. It happens to everyone. Correct the problem and return to being a person of good character.

CHAPTER TWO

You Can't Surge Trust

The people when rightly
and fully trusted will return
the trust.

—ABRAHAM LINCOLN

I parked in the small lot at the front of CIA headquarters. Dressed in my navy blue uniform, I got out, walked up the stairs and into the large headquarters building. Emblazoned on the floor was the crest of the Central Intelligence Agency: a circle with a blue background and, in the middle, a white shield with a red starburst, above which was an eagle, his head turned to his right. To my left was the Memorial Wall, with 137 stars commemorating the CIA officers who had been killed in the line of duty. Below it was the Book of Honor with the names of the fallen. In all the years that I had come to the CIA, I had never ceased to be moved by the simple marble edifice and the individual stars that carried with them such sacrifice.

As I approached the guard, I could see my escort standing behind the desk, waiting for me to swipe my badge and get past the entry point.

"Sir, good to see you again," she said as I pushed past the turnstile. "The director is waiting for you in his office."

As commander of a special operations unit, I had been brought back to CIA headquarters to meet the new director of CIA, Leon Panetta.

We took a sharp left into a small corridor and walked onto the director's private elevator. My escort pushed the button, and we went directly to the seventh floor, with the elevator opening into Panetta's outer office.

There another escort met me and showed me to the waiting room.

He smiled, offered me a cup of coffee, and said politely, "The director will be with you in just a few moments."

As I waited, in my mind I went through what I knew about Leon Panetta. A child of Italian immigrants, he was born and raised in Monterey, California, on a walnut farm. He attended Santa Clara University and went on to get a law degree from the same school. Panetta spent a short time in the Army and then had an incredibly distinguished career as an eight-time congressman, director of the Office of Management and Budget, and chief of staff for President Bill Clinton. Panetta was known for his infectious laugh, warm personality, and wickedly sharp intellect. He was outwardly gregarious but inwardly tenacious. But with all his Washington experience, I knew that being director of the CIA was completely different from anything Panetta had done before. Moreover, the military and the CIA sometimes had a love-hate relationship. We were always competing for resources, missions, and talent. I was about to find out which side of that relationship Leon Panetta was on.

A few minutes later I was called into his office. As I walked in the door, Panetta, a big grin on his face, his hand extended in friendship, said, "I'm Leon Panetta, so very good to meet you!"

"It's a pleasure to meet you as well, Mr. Director."

"Oh please," Panetta said. "Call me Leon."

I laughed. "I'm sorry, sir. I've been in the military too long—that's not going to happen."

He laughed along with me.

Standing in the room, arrayed in an informal semicircle, were all of the CIA's senior officers. Panetta motioned me to the first man in line and introduced him as the director of operations (DDO). The DDO had a slight grin on his face and a twinkle in his eye as he nodded to me, and I nodded back. Next down the line was the director of analysis. Then Panetta introduced me to each of the regional and functional directors. I politely shook hands as I walked down the line.

When I had met everyone, Panetta invited me to take a seat at his conference table.

"Thanks again for coming to visit, Bill. I think the relationship between the CIA and your command is very important, and I wanted you to meet my senior leadership team so we could begin to build some trust in each other."

"Thank you, sir," I replied. "But…" I hesitated to continue.

"But," chuckled the director of operations, "Bill and I have known each other since 2003 in Baghdad." Then the director of the Counterterrorism Center chimed in: "Bill and I spent a year together in Afghanistan." That was followed by each of the directors recounting our previous experiences together: Yemen, Somalia, North Africa, Saudi Arabia, Kuwait, Egypt, Pakistan, and the Philippines.

Panetta roared with laughter. "So, am I the only one who hasn't served with you?"

I smiled.

"Well sir, most of us have grown up together fighting this war on terrorism."

"Well, good then." Panetta smiled. "We won't have to spend time getting to know each other. Because when *it* hits the fan, we won't have time to build trust."

A year later, I would be called back into Panetta's office, but this time to help plan the raid to get Osama bin Laden. President Obama had given Leon Panetta the task of capturing or killing bin Laden. The mission could easily have gone to another unit within the CIA. The decision by the CIA to use my special operations forces did not come in a flash. It was the result of years of working together, years of building personal and professional relationships, years of earning each other's trust. And even when we had interagency squabbles, of which there were many, the CIA believed they could trust me and they could trust my team.

In 2014 I retired from the military, and in January of 2015 I became the chancellor of the University of Texas System. The system comprised fourteen different campuses, over 230,000 students, and 100,000 employees. As the first "nontraditional" chancellor (a person with no academic background), I was a bit suspect to the faculty and the system staff. I had no previous relationship with any of the campus presidents and had been out of Texas for almost forty years. While everyone seemed to appreciate my military career, they still had doubts as to whether I was the right man for the job. As with any new undertaking, I knew that I would have to earn their trust. But after years of finding myself in similar situations, I had the formula down pat. Show up early. Work hard. Stay late. Have a plan. Deliver on your promises. Share the hardships with the employees. Show that you care. Admit your mistakes. And—did I mention?—work hard.

In his book *The Speed of Trust*, Stephen Covey says there are two components to trust: character and competence. You may initially trust someone if you know them to be a man or woman of sound character. But if that person fails to deliver on their promises, if they are shown to be incompetent in handling the affairs of the business, then after a while you lose trust in them. As a leader your competence can and will be measured in your personal behavior, your professional demeanor, your effectiveness in handling problems, and your consistency.

To be a great leader you must be trusted by your employees. If they do not trust you, they will not follow you. It takes time to build trust, but it is time well spent if you intend to lead effectively.

It's Simple:

1. Engage with your employees on a personal level to show them you are a leader of good character, a trustworthy individual.
2. Only promise what you can deliver. The quickest way to lose trust is to overpromise and underdeliver.
3. Know that trust is built over time. Don't rush it.

CHAPTER THREE

When in Command, Command

Life is not easy for any of us. But what of that? We must have perseverance and above all confidence in ourselves. We must believe that we are gifted for something and that this thing must be attained.

—MARIE CURIE

I sat with my back straight, head erect, listening to Lieutenant Jim McCoy as he paced across the front of the classroom lecturing the thirty midshipmen on the Battle of Midway. Naval History was a required course for all freshman officer candidates at the University of Texas. We started with the Peloponnesian War, "crossed the T" with Lord Nelson at the Battle of Trafalgar, fought with Admiral Jellicoe at Jutland, launched off the USS *Yorktown* at the Battle of the Coral Sea, and now we were preparing for one of the biggest naval engagements of WWII, Midway.

The time was June 1942, just seven months after the bombing at Pearl Harbor. The Imperial Japanese Navy, realizing their mistake in not destroying the American carrier fleet at Pearl, were setting a trap off the island of Midway. Although 1,300 nautical miles from Oahu, Midway was a strategic base for the Americans. Japanese admiral Yamamoto believed that if the U.S. Navy felt that the island was threatened, they would sail their carriers from Pearl Harbor to protect this important base. He was right.

Yamamoto intended to lure the carriers into a fight by concealing most of his naval force, making it seem as though the Americans had a numerical advantage. What Yamamoto didn't know was that the Americans had broken the Japanese code and were able to partially decipher the Imperial Navy's plan. But even with that partial plan, there was a lot of doubt as to whether the U.S. Navy was up for the fight. The Battle of the Coral Sea had almost destroyed the USS *Yorktown*, and the Navy's most experienced admiral, Bull Halsey, was hospitalized with shingles. The military leadership in Washington was against sailing the fleet to defend Midway, but ultimately the decision to meet the Japanese at Midway would rest with the commander of the Pacific Fleet, Admiral Chester Nimitz.

Lieutenant McCoy reached for a plastic viewgraph and placed it on the projector. He flipped off the lights and on the screen was a picture of Admiral Nimitz. Nimitz had a prominent head of white hair, steel-blue eyes fixed into the distance, and a thin, serious smile, all framed in his navy blue uniform with the five gold stripes of a fleet admiral. McCoy proudly told us that Nimitz was of German stock, born and raised in Fredericksburg, Texas, not far from where we were in Austin. He had attended the United States Naval Academy, graduating with honors.

McCoy paused momentarily, wondering whether he should recount the next part of Nimitz's history. He continued, explaining that as a young officer, Ensign Nimitz had been in command of the destroyer *Decatur* when the *Decatur* ran aground off the Philippines in 1908. Nimitz was court-martialed for dereliction of duty, but only received a letter of reprimand because of his stellar performance up to that point. Nimitz's character would be shaped by the grounding incident in the Philippines. He knew that with command comes great responsibility, but also that with command comes the need to be decisive and accept that you might not always get it right. Nimitz would go on to serve in the submarine fleet during WWI and then rise through the ranks to become commander of the Pacific Fleet in WWII.

In the spring of 1942, the intelligence on the Japanese intentions at Midway was anything but solid. Many in the admiral's own ranks questioned the strategic benefit of trying to save Midway. And even more officers feared that an American defeat at Midway would mean a quick Japanese victory in the Pacific. The ramifications of a bad decision were calamitous, but the ramification of no decision might be an existential disaster.

Nimitz reviewed the intelligence, consulted with his staff, and talked with his commanders, but the ultimate decision was his. He anguished over the decision for days. What would happen if he were wrong? Thousands of sailors might die. Thousands more would perish in fighting on Midway and the island chains leading to Japan. The fate of the entire Navy, and perhaps our nation, rested on this decision.

Legend has it that during a conversation with Admiral Bull Halsey, Nimitz confessed his apprehension. The weight of the decision about Midway was overwhelming him. Halsey, blunt as ever, reminded the admiral of Nimitz's own personal conviction.

"You once told me," Halsey began, "that when in command, *command.*"

It was the clarion call that Nimitz needed. He understood that commanders are expected to make the tough decision. To act with purpose. To be confident and lead from the front. To accept the challenge and steel yourself for the rough waters ahead. A commander must command. Command the situation. Command the troops. Command your fears. Take command.

On June 4, 1942, Naval Air Forces launched from the USS *Yorktown*, the USS *Enterprise*, and the USS *Hornet* and engaged the Japanese fleet off Midway. In the ensuing two days, four Japanese carriers were sunk, and the Americans lost the *Enterprise*. But history would show that the Battle of Midway was the single most decisive naval battle of the war and turned the tide in the Pacific.

Lieutenant McCoy finished the lesson on Midway. He turned on the lights and looked out across the room of young midshipmen dressed in our white naval uniforms.

"One day," he said, "some of you might be lucky enough to command. Maybe you will command a ship or a submarine or a squadron. And if that day comes, you will find command the most rewarding but also the most challenging time of your career."

He glanced out the window and paused for a moment.

"Never forget that as a commander you will be expected to lead. If you are chosen for the job, take it with some humility, but also accept the fact that you're good or you wouldn't be commanding."

He grinned. "Who knows? Maybe someday one of you will be an admiral, and like Nimitz you will have the opportunity to lead our great sailors during time of war."

We all laughed. Still in our teens, fighting acne, and

only hoping to pass our first semester of college, being an admiral was the furthest thing from our minds.

Thirty-eight years later, as a four-star admiral and commander of the U.S. Special Operations Command, I walked into my office in Tampa to find a new desk waiting for me. I was a bit confused, as the old desk had seemed perfectly fine. When I inquired about the desk, my administrative assistant, Senior Master Sergeant Dana Hughes, smiled and said, "Well sir, we thought this might be a better fit for you."

Perplexed, I looked at the desk again. It was older than I first realized, a large executive-style desk with deep-grain wood and leather side panels. As I approached the desk, there was a small, framed picture resting on the edge. The man in the picture was unmistakable. It was Admiral Chester Nimitz, and this was his desk. The Navy Archives had been kind enough to loan it to SOCOM for my use. I was humbled beyond all measure.

For the next three years, I sat at that desk, and whenever I thought I had some difficult days, I would remember where I was sitting. I would remember the lives that hung in the balance, the decisions that affected millions, the sense of loss and the sense of victory that Nimitz must have felt. And on those days when I felt indecisive, when

I took too much counsel of my fears, when worry threatened to stall my actions, I hearkened back to Nimitz's words: "When in command, command!" And with those words as my guide, I always tried to do right by the men and women who served with me.

———

Being a leader, whether you are the CEO, the admiral, the general, the chairperson, or the director for an office of two, is difficult. As a leader you must always appear to be in command, even on those days when you struggle with the pressures of the job. You must be confident. You must be decisive. You must smile. You must laugh. You must engage with your employees and be thankful for their work. You must have the look of a person in charge. You must instill in your men and women a sense of pride that *their* leader can handle any problem.

As a leader you can't have a bad day. You must never look beaten, no matter the circumstance. If you sulk, if you hang your head, if you whine or complain about the leaders above you or the followers below you, then you will lose the respect of your men and women, and the attitude of despair will spread like wildfire.

Being a leader is an awesome responsibility. There are days when it can be frightening to know that the fate of the organization rests on your shoulders. But you must also realize that you were chosen to be the leader because you have proven yourself along the way. You have demonstrated that you know the business. You have shown that you can handle the pressures and be decisive. You have exhibited all the qualities necessary to lead. And even if none of the above holds true, now that you are the leader, you are in command. So, take the damn helm and command!

It's Simple:

1. Be confident. You were given the job because you have talent and experience. Trust your instincts.
2. Be decisive. Don't take too much counsel of your fears. Be thoughtful, but not paralyzed by indecision.
3. Be passionate. Show your employees you care about them and about the mission.

CHAPTER FOUR

We All Have Our Frog Floats

True humility is not an abject, groveling, self-despising spirit; it is but a right estimate of ourselves as God sees us.

—TRYON EDWARDS, AMERICAN THEOLOGIAN

The oncoming boat was barreling down on me, its bow creating a wake of white foam and churning blue water. In the small cockpit I could see the helmsman, his eyes flashing between me and the tiny inflatable raft secured to the port side of the craft. In the raft, another man, holding a thick rubber loop, his arms extended ready to catch me in the sling as the boat sped by.

Twenty-five yards and closing.

The boat was almost on me.

I could hear the man in the raft yelling, "Kick, kick hard, now!"

"Kick, kick, kick," I yelled to myself, my fins pushing hard against the bay water.

Ten yards.

Five yards.

Now, now!

Inside the raft I could see the slingman straining to reach me. Kicking as hard as I could, I thrust my arm into the loop and the momentum from the boat and a hard tug from the slingman yanked me into the raft. Quickly pulling my arm out of the sling, I rolled to one side of the raft and then climbed aboard the boat. Right behind me, another frogman was ripped out of the water and into the raft. Within minutes the entire platoon had been recovered and was aboard the boat.

This was real frogman stuff. Small boat cast and recovery. Just like our frogman ancestors had done at Tarawa, Okinawa, Tinian, and countless other islands in the Pacific. And to think, they were paying me to do this.

After we finished the evolution, the patrol boat pulled into the pier at the Naval Amphibious Base, Coronado, and we started offloading our gear.

"Hey, Mr. Mac! Mr. Mac!" came a familiar voice from down the pier.

It was Petty Officer Larry L. Jones, my senior enlisted man in the communications shop.

"Double L, what's up?"

"Sir, the skipper wants to see you," he said, a bit out of breath.

"Me?"

"Yes sir. You."

I didn't even know the commanding officer knew who I

was. As the brand-new ensign at Underwater Demolition Team Eleven (UDT-11), I tried to keep a low profile. I had met the skipper, shaken his hand, seen him at an occasional officers' call, but certainly didn't see any reason he would single me out for anything.

But, I thought...I had been making a good impression on the other officers and the senior enlisted. I took my training seriously. I worked hard. I PT'd hard. I stayed late. I listened to the seasoned Vietnam vets.

Yeah, maybe I had been singled out for something special.

There had been some rumor that we were planning a real-world mission. Maybe this was it! Maybe it was a mission to snatch some terrorist from the Balkans. Maybe it was a swimmer sneak attack into Vladivostok or an across-the-beach mission into North Korea to take out a missile site.

"Okay, Double L. I need to get back to the team and change into my khakis."

"No time, sir. The skipper said he has to meet with the commodore ASAP and wanted to talk to you right now."

"The commodore?" *The man in charge of all the SEALs and Frogs on the West Coast.* The Big Kahuna. This must be important!

We hopped into Jones's truck, sped through the naval

base, crossed Highway 1, and drove onto the UDT-11 compound.

Ripping off my shorty wet suit, I brushed my hair back with my hand, tucked my blue-and-gold T-shirt into my khaki swim trunks, and walked into the headquarters building.

The skipper's yeoman stood up as I walked in.

"Are you Ensign McRaven?"

"I am."

"Have a seat. I'll let the CO know you're here."

I sat down on the brown Naugahyde couch and gazed at the pictures on the wall. There were World War II photos of frogmen clearing Pacific Island beaches for the amphibious landings; pictures of web-footed warriors, clad in thick rubber dry suits, climbing the rocks on a Korean beach; men, dive masks on their heads and fins on their feet, welcoming the Apollo 11 crew back from the first moon landing; and SEALs, bandoliers of ammunition slung across their chests, wading into chest-deep mud in the Mekong Delta. I was part of an elite force, and man it felt good!

The petty officer returned.

"Sir, the skipper will see you now."

I combed my wet hair over one more time and walked

into the office. Sitting behind the desk was Commander Bill Salisbury, the skipper of Underwater Demolition Team Eleven. A highly decorated Vietnam-era SEAL, he had welcomed me to the team a few weeks earlier with a warm smile and a strong handshake. I liked the guy even though we hadn't spent much time together.

I came to attention and announced, "Sir, Ensign McRaven reporting as requested."

Salisbury smiled. My junior-officer enthusiasm was maybe a bit too much.

"Relax, Mr. McRaven."

"Yes sir," I said, coming to parade rest.

"The XO tells me you've hit the ground running."

"Thank you, sir."

"You're making a good impression on the wardroom and the Chief's locker."

I nodded and swelled with pride.

"The commodore called me earlier today and he asked me who my best ensign was."

I swelled even larger—if that was possible.

"He's got something he wants you to do. And if it's important to the commodore, then it's important."

"Yes sir!" I said too loudly.

Here it comes, I thought. A mission. This is why I went

through SEAL training. Maybe someday I'll find myself in one of those pictures out front.

Salisbury paused for effect.

"Every year, the city of Coronado holds a Fourth of July parade. We haven't participated in a long while," he said.

Okay. I'm confused. Must be something I'm missing.

"So, this year the commodore wants to have a Frog Float, and I need you to take charge of building the float." He smiled.

"A Frog Float?" I asked.

"Yes, you know. A big green Freddie the Frog, puffing on a cigar, carrying a stick of dynamite. The folks in Coronado will love it!"

"Yes sir," I responded with a lot less enthusiasm.

"Well, check with the supply officer. He can get you all the material you need for the float. That's all, Mr. McRaven. Thanks very much."

As I stood there a bit stunned, Salisbury went back to reading his daily message traffic.

I slowly turned around and walked out of the office. As I passed the action pictures on the wall, I somehow doubted my Frog Float would ever make the cut.

Frustrated, I headed to the locker room to change clothes and get back to work. As I sat on the bench, muttering profanities under my breath, I heard a deep raspy voice from the locker behind me.

"What's the matter, Ensign?"

I turned around to see Master Chief Hershel Davis, the senior enlisted man from our sister team, UDT-12. Davis was the personification of a frogman—tall, lean, tan, with a ruddy face, steel-gray eyes, and huge handlebar mustache. He had seen more combat action than any ten men I knew.

"Nothing important, Master Chief."

"Uh-huh," he said in a fatherly tone as he took a seat beside me.

Why did I feel like I was in the confessional?

I confessed.

"Skipper just called me into his office and told me he wants me to take charge of building..." I paused. "Building the Frog Float for the Fourth of July parade."

"Hmm," the Master Chief grunted. "And my guess is— you would rather be out jumping out of airplanes, locking out of submarines, going on a mission to save the world."

"Exactly right!" Again, too loud.

"Let me tell you something, Ensign. I've been in this Canoe Club for almost thirty years. Sooner or later we all

41

have to do things we don't want to do. But if you're going to do it, then do it right. Build the best damn Frog Float you can!"

And there it was. *"Build the best damn Frog Float you can!"*

Throughout the rest of my career, I would be asked to build a lot of "frog floats." Asked to do those menial tasks that no one else wanted, those tasks that seemed beneath the "dignity of my rank." But each time, I remembered the words of the master chief and tried to do the best I could, to be proud of whatever job I was given. I found, in my career, that if you took pride in the little jobs, people would think you worthy of the bigger jobs.

On July 4, 1978, the UDT Frog Float was awarded top prize in its category, and the picture of my "first mission" hung proudly in the UDT-11 compound for years afterward.

It's Simple:

1. Be humble in your demeanor and your expectations.
2. Accept the fact that you will be asked to do jobs that are beneath your status. Do them to the best of your ability.
3. Measure the strength of your employees by their willingness to do the little tasks and do them well.

CHAPTER FIVE

The Only Easy Day Was Yesterday

It isn't enough to believe
in something; you have to
have the stamina to meet
the obstacles and
overcome them.

—GOLDA MEIR

The sound of the bell echoed across the asphalt Grinder. One, two, three rings as the deep brass tone bounced off the buildings and into the collective consciousness of the SEAL trainees doing morning calisthenics. Out of the corner of my eye I watched as Petty Officer Halliday took off his helmet and placed it at the base of the bell. The SEAL instructor, dressed in a blue-and-gold T-shirt with khaki swim trunks and green jungle boots, said something unintelligible. All I caught was Halliday yelling at the top of his voice, "Hooyah, Instructor Faketty!" Faketty said something else and Halliday turned and ran back to the barracks. We would never see Halliday again. With three rings of the bell, he had just quit SEAL training.

Two weeks earlier we had completed Hell Week. Arguably the toughest week in any military training, Hell Week was six days of no sleep, constant harassment by the instructors, and always being kept cold, wet, and miserable. Like all of us, Halliday had experienced the euphoria of completed the grueling trial. He knew that in the ...ory of SEAL training, most students dropped out during that week. But he had made it, and in his mind the rest of training was going to be much easier. He could see graduation on the horizon. He could envision the SEAL Trident being placed on his chest. He had dreams of joining an elite team of professionals and having the adventure of a lifetime. He could taste victory. I know this because in his euphoria he had confided in me his vision of the future.

But Halliday failed to remember the words that were etched on a large wooden sign that hung behind the instructor's PT stand. The sign read THE ONLY EASY DAY WAS YESTERDAY. It had become the SEALs' mantra since it was first written on the back of T-shirts worn by SEAL training class 89. *The Only Easy Day Was Yesterday.* The words were self-explanatory, but the meaning went much deeper. The words were a cautionary tale to every SEAL trainee. They said, "If you think the hard part is over, you're mistaken." Tomorrow will be just as difficult as today, maybe more so. But the words carried great weight outside training as well. To me the words were a clarion call, a reminder that every day required my full effort. They reminded me that no day was going to be easy and that as a leader I must be prepared to give it my all. Every. Single. Day.

In 1986, Congress passed the Goldwater-Nichols Act, which reorganized the Defense Department, and with that came the Nunn-Cohen Amendment, which established the United States Special Operations Command (USSOCOM). These two congressional mandates forever changed the military, and special operations in particular. One of the officers who led the charge to establish USSOCOM was Navy captain Irve Charles "Chuck" LeMoyne. LeMoyne was a Vietnam-era SEAL who had risen to the top of the SEAL ranks and helped shepherd the bill through Congress and then implement it in the Navy. LeMoyne had a mixed reputation around the Teams. He didn't fit the Vietnam-era SEAL profile. Instead of being rowdy and tough-talking, LeMoyne was very proper, soft-spoken, and quietly determined.

After the establishment of USSOCOM, LeMoyne was promoted to admiral and was the first commander of Naval Special Warfare Command. He was the first SEAL to fill an admiral's billet within the SEAL community. I'm sure he hoped his toughest days were behind him. But instead of settling for his admiral's star, LeMoyne completely reorganized the SEALs and Special Boat Units and set the community up for long-term success. It was a monumental task and one that came with constant criticism from within the SEAL community and from without. But in all my time around Admiral Chuck LeMoyne, I never once saw him frustrated, flustered, or beaten down. No matter what challenges confronted him, he was always the man in charge. He understood that all eyes were on him and that no matter the circumstances, he had a responsibility to put on a good face.

After being promoted to two-star admiral, Chuck LeMoyne was diagnosed with throat cancer, possibly the result of his exposure to Agent Orange in Vietnam. But instead of retiring or retreating from helping the SEALs, he doubled down. When his vocal cords were removed and he was given an electronic speech aid, he continued to do public speaking. As the senior active-duty SEAL, LeMoyne was the Bull Frog at the time, and I recall every speech began with a humorous line about his digitally enhanced "croaking voice." When I asked him once how he was able to carry on despite the cancer, he smiled, put the speech aid up to his neck, and said, "The only easy day..." He didn't have to finish the line.

Sadly, in 1997, Chuck LeMoyne passed away at the age of fifty-seven. He never fully realized the impact he had on today's Navy SEALs and Special Boat Units and on those young officers, like me, who watched him lead with grace, humility, humor, and courage.

Years later, in 2002, when I was serving in the Bush White House, the commander of the East Coast SEALs invited me down for a conference. As was typical of a SEAL gathering, we started each day with an hour of calisthenics followed by a long run. Having survived a serious parachute accident in 2001, my body had still not healed, and trying to do any physical training was challenging at best. But I thought of Chuck LeMoyne and I knew he wouldn't quit because of a little discomfort. So I manned up and joined the group for morning PT. We started with the usual series of push-ups, sit-ups, eight-count body builders, and flutter kicks. I could barely manage any of the exercises but tried to tough it out. Upon completion of the calisthenics, we began a ten-mile run.

All my fellow SEALs started off in a sprint. I was only able to keep up for the first hundred yards and then began to fall back. Within a few minutes I couldn't even see the pack anymore. The course was five laps around a two-mile stretch of state park. As the minutes passed and I lumbered along, the first runner, a young SEAL lieutenant, began to lap me. Slowing momentarily, he pulled up beside me and, knowing about my parachute accident, gave me a penetrating and confused look.

"Sir, what the hell are you doing?" he asked.

"What do you mean?" I responded.

He shook his head and said, "Sir, why are you even out here? You don't have anything left to prove."

Before I could answer, he bolted away and ran off into the distance.

I was a Navy SEAL captain at the time. I had already completed my Major Command, an important milestone in an officer's career, and to this young lieutenant, I had nothing left to prove. But what I wanted to tell him— what I wanted to yell at the top of my voice—*was how very wrong he was*.

The day you no longer believe you have something to prove, the day you no longer believe you must give it your all, the day you think you are entitled to special treatment, the day you think all your hard days are behind you, is the day you are *no longer* the right leader for the job.

Leadership requires energy. It requires stamina. It requires resilience. It requires everything you have and then some. The men and women that work for you will feed off your energy. If you look unprepared to deal with the challenges of the day, they will see this. If you look beaten down because today was harder than yesterday, they will feel this. If you are not prepared to give it your all, they will know this. And if you think this is just about leaders in combat, you're mistaken. This is about every great leader who was given a difficult task and asked to inspire, motivate, and manage the people under their charge.

But it doesn't mean that every day has to exhaust you. Being a great leader doesn't mean you have to have superhuman strength. It only means that you have to recognize that it will require effort, every day. And some days you just won't bring it. That's okay. That's normal. But then, bring it the next day, or the next. You will only fail as a leader when you think that today is going to be easier than yesterday.

It's Simple:

1. You must bring energy and enthusiasm every single day.
2. You are not entitled to anything but more hard work. The rank and file are working hard and getting paid less.
3. Attack each day as though it were critical to the organization's success.

CHAPTER SIX

Run to the Sound of the Guns

The great corporations of
this country were not
founded by ordinary
people. They were founded
by people with
extraordinary intelligence,
ambition, and
aggressiveness.

—DANIEL PATRICK
MOYNIHAN

Paris in the fall is beautiful. The trees along the Champs-Élysées are just turning. The morning is crisp and the aroma of strong coffee and warm French pastries drifts through the air. At night they light up the Eiffel Tower, and the crowds of young and old alike snuggle under its large steel beams for both warmth and companionship. There is just something magical about Paris, particularly when you're thinking about it from Afghanistan.

I had been dreaming about Paris for months. I was getting a few days' leave from operations in Afghanistan, just enough time to fly to France and back. My wife, Georgeann, and daughter, Kelly, were scheduled to meet me there, and after six months without them, I was aching to see them. Then came a knock at my door.

"Enter," I yelled across the plywood room.

The door to my small B-Hut opened and in walked the colonel in charge of the night's combat operations.

"Sir, sorry to bother you, but we've had a civilian-casualty incident and it's not pretty."

"Grab a chair," I said.

The colonel pulled out a map and some overhead photos and laid them on the small table in my room. Over the next few minutes, he outlined the actions on the objectives that had led to the civilian casualties. He was right, it wasn't pretty. The loss of civilians was always hard—innocent people caught in the crossfire or mistaken for Taliban or al Qaeda. You try to tell yourself it is the nature of war, but that never makes it easier. They are real people who have suffered real loss. Nothing ever quite eases the pain—not theirs and not yours.

"Sir, the general has been notified, and needless to say, he's not happy. I told his staff that you were heading out tomorrow, and he has asked to talk with you tonight before you departed on leave."

"Alright. Set up the call. I'll be up in the JOC momentarily."

As the colonel departed, I already knew what had to be done.

I picked up the phone and, working through the military operator, I placed a call to our home in Fort Bragg, North Carolina.

As the phone rang on the other end, Georgeann immediately picked up. Before I could even speak, she said, "Is everything okay? We just can't wait to see you in Paris!"

I paused. She knew before I could even get the words out. "You're not coming to Paris, are you?"

I took a deep breath and explained the situation. There was just no way I could leave at that moment. At that moment—with the tragic loss of life, when the reputation of the organization was at risk, when those above me and below me were looking for leadership, when my presence was necessary to face the crisis—there was no way I could fly off to Paris. I knew it, and after thirty-five years of marriage, she knew it as well. We had been here before. It was a lesson I had learned many times over in my career. When things go bad, that is the time for a leader to be aggressive, to move to where the problem is and address the crisis head-on.

———

The temperature in early July of 1863 was stifling. The soldiers of the 20th Maine Infantry Regiment were exhausted from days of hard marching to a small town in Pennsylvania called Gettysburg. Intelligence indicated that

General Robert E. Lee was moving his army from Virginia across the Potomac into Pennsylvania to cut off the Union forces from their capital in Washington, D.C.

A small Union contingent had arrived a few days earlier and positioned itself at McPherson's Ridge, a key piece of terrain west of Gettysburg. When the first Confederates arrived, they were surprised to see Union troops already holding ground. Over the next two days both the Union army, now under the command of General George Meade, and the Confederate army reinforced their positions around Gettysburg, with the Union forces being arrayed along the high ground referred to as Cemetery Ridge.

Cemetery Ridge extended from Culp's Hill in the north, down the ridge and south toward Big and Little Round Tops. Little Round Top was the far-left flank of the Union lines and the most vulnerable to Rebel attacks. If the Confederates could take Little Round Top, they could sweep through the Union lines and defeat Meade's army.

On July 2, 1863, the battle had begun, and several attempts by the Rebel forces to break through the lines at Cemetery Ridge had already been repelled. At one point, to reinforce a weakening Union position farther north, General John Geary moved a substantial portion of his men away from Little Round Top, leaving the left flank severely exposed. When Meade discovered the mistake, he immediately sent a brigade from the 1st Division to buttress his sagging defenses.

Lee, however, saw an opening, and before the Union brigade could be fully arrayed along the ridge, he ordered an attack. Holding Little Round Top were men from the 2nd United States Sharpshooters, soldiers from the 16th Michigan, the 44th New York, and the 83rd Pennsylvania, and at the very end of the left flank were 386 infantrymen of the 20th Maine under the command of Colonel Joshua Chamberlain.

Chamberlain was not your quintessential soldier. Just prior to the war, he had been a professor of modern language at Bowdoin College. A highly sophisticated, cultured, and somewhat sedentary individual, he was a student of military history, and when the war broke out, he volunteered. He was given command of the 20th Maine, which was not considered one of the premier units in the army. In fact, most of the unit was made up of unwilling soldiers, mutineers, and two-year conscripts. Over the months that followed, Chamberlain did everything he could to get the 20th Maine into fighting shape.

On July 2, a numerically superior force of Major General John B. Hood's division began to attack the Maine troops.

Hood had ordered his soldiers to find the Union left, turn it, and capture Little Round Top.

As the battle raged and the Confederate soldiers seemed poised to defeat the smaller 20th Maine, Chamberlain, from his position higher on the ridge, grabbed his rifle and moved forward to the regimental line. Wounded from a previous cannon shell, Chamberlain limped toward his men, aligned himself with the regimental flag, and yelled, "Bayonet! Forward to the right!" Executing a right-wheel maneuver, the soldiers of the 20th Maine fixed their bayonets and charged down the hill into the oncoming Rebel force. The level of ferocity and courage displayed by the 20th Maine was so surprising that it forced the Confederates to retreat, saving Little Round Top and the left flank of the Union forces.

History would later record that Chamberlain's leadership that day and the courage of the enlisted soldiers of the 20th Maine saved the Union forces at Gettysburg. And, had Meade been defeated at Gettysburg, it is possible the South would have won the Civil War. Imagine how different the world would be today if Chamberlain had not "run to the sound of the guns."

———

Unfortunately, not all leaders understand this concept of moving quickly to address the problem, of accepting responsibility and making themselves the face of the solution. In April of 2010, when the oil rig Deepwater Horizon exploded in the Gulf of Mexico, killing eleven men and creating one of the largest oil spills in the history of the industry, the parent company was slow to react. The CEO initially stayed in London rather than moving to the U.S. Gulf Coast, where the damage had occurred. Worse, even though the incident caused billions of dollars of damage and disrupted the lives of millions of people, the CEO downplayed the magnitude of the incident, claiming the spill was "tiny" compared to a "very large ocean." Instead of accepting responsibility and confronting the issue head-on, he became exasperated as the disaster continued to dominate the headlines and, more importantly to him, it began to impact *his* life. At one point he told a reporter, "You know, I'd like my life back." Needless to say, in light of all the other lives ruined by the explosion, his tone-deaf response didn't land well. He was out as the CEO soon thereafter.

———

Why is there a reluctance to be the face of the solution? Because if you are going to be the face of the solution, it likely means you had a hand in the problem. Good leaders understand that organizations are going to have challenges. That's why you were hired to lead. Embrace the challenge. Accept the fact that you must attack each problem with vigor and that sometimes only you, the leader, can solve the most vexing of institutional crises. Never shy away. Never retreat from a difficult problem.

———

My boss in Afghanistan was not happy about the civilian casualties, nor should he have been. Fortunately, he was a great soldier, and he understood the challenges of combat. It took my organization a long time to earn back the trust of my superiors and, more importantly, the trust of local civilians and our Afghan colleagues. But the first step was accepting responsibility for the tragedy and then aggressively addressing the problem. Running to the sound of the guns is always risky, both personally and professionally, but hiding from the problem will only make it worse. Sometimes you just have to "fix bayonets" and charge into the breach.

It's Simple:

1. Be aggressive. When you see a problem, do something about it. That's what is expected of leaders.
2. Move to a place where you can best assess the nature of the problem and provide guidance and resources to resolve it as quickly as possible.
3. Communicate your intent every step of the way.

CHAPTER SEVEN

Sua Sponte

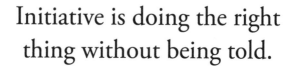

Initiative is doing the right
thing without being told.

—VICTOR HUGO

Hill 205 seemed an unlikely place for an Army legend to be born. After MacArthur's landing at Inchon on September 15, 1950, U.S. forces began to rout the North Korean army, pushing them well above the 38th parallel, almost to the Yalu River on the border with China. With the success of the Americans and the collapse of the North Koreans, some experts believed the war would be over soon.

As the 25th Infantry Division pressed the fight toward the Kuryong River in the north, victory seemed imminent. But to the surprise of MacArthur and the U.S. military, Chinese intervention would change all of that. On November 25, 1950, a small contingent of Army Rangers were directed to take and hold a vital piece of terrain just south of the river. Unbeknownst to them, the Chinese 39th Army had massed a huge force to defend the hill.

The Rangers, led by First Lieutenant Ralph Puckett, began to make their way across an open field toward the high ground that was Hill 205. As the Rangers maneuvered toward the hill, the Chinese opened up with a barrage of mortars, machine gun and small arms fire. With his men completely exposed, Puckett called in American artillery to suppress the incoming mortar rounds, but the Chinese machine gunners and mortarmen were camouflaged in gun pits and hard to locate. He had to find a way to pinpoint the Chinese gunners before the Rangers could return accurate fire.

Puckett, who had positioned himself at the front of the advancing Rangers, knew there was only one thing he could do. With complete disregard for his own life, Ralph Puckett rose from his foxhole and dashed out into the open field, forcing the Chinese to take aim at the young lieutenant. As the machine gunners began to fire at the sprinting Puckett, the Rangers spotted their positions and engaged them. Puckett returned to his foxhole only to catch his breath, and then leaped out and ran into the open again and then again. With each dash by Puckett into the exposed terrain, the Rangers were able to isolate and destroy more enemy machine gunners.

Having suppressed the small arms fire, the Rangers proceeded to take Hill 205. History would show that over the next two days, the Rangers under the command of Ralph Puckett would fight off wave after wave of Chinese assaults that took the lives of ten Rangers and left thirty-one wounded, including Puckett. For his actions leading up to and capturing Hill 205, Ralph Puckett would be awarded the Medal of Honor. Puckett would go on to serve in Vietnam, where he would receive the nation's second-highest honor, the Distinguished Service Cross, and two Silver Stars.

Years later, when recalling the heroism of Lieutenant Puckett running across the open field, one of his soldiers said, "It needed to be done and someone needed to do it!"

The Rangers have a Latin saying, *Sua Sponte*. It means, *Of Your Own Accord*. In other words, doing what needs to be done, without being told to do so. There is often the misguided belief that soldiers only follow orders, but the strength of the American military is that the great soldiers, the truly great leaders, do what is right without being told. They do what is right to protect their men and women. They do what is right to uphold the reputation of their unit. They do what is right to bring honor to their country. They do what needs to be done, whether ordered to do so or not. This sense of initiative separates the great leaders from the mediocre ones. No one ordered Ralph Puckett to run with reckless abandon into the open field, but *someone had to do it*.

I saw this level of initiative time and again during the

wars in Iraq and Afghanistan. The Army, Navy, Air Force, and Marine Corps understood that the nature of the fight required the generals and the admirals to allow the junior officers and enlisted to make tough combat decisions. We had to delegate responsibility because there just weren't enough senior officers to oversee all the tactical operations. We had to trust the rank and file to do the right thing.

It is always difficult for senior leaders to trust their subordinates with important decisions, decisions that invariably affect the reputation of the unit and that of the senior leader. But if you don't create a culture that allows the rank and file to act on their own, they will be mired in indecisiveness that will stall any forward momentum.

However, leadership is not always defined by the man or the woman at the top of the chain of command, and you don't always have to be in command to lead.

———

It was a typical day in Honolulu: The skies were clear, a warm tropical breeze gently brushed the palm trees, and the water off Ford Island was a majestic blue. As a Navy captain and the "commodore" of Naval Special Warfare Group ONE, I had come to Ford Island, Hawaii, in 1998 to dedicate a building in honor of my close friend Lieutenant Commander Moki Martin. Moki was born and raised in Hawaii and had gone on to have a remarkable career as a Navy SEAL. A Vietnam veteran, Moki was the quintessential frogman. During his career, he was a highly decorated combat warrior, an expert with every weapon in the armory, an amazing skydiver and scuba diver, and an exceptional athlete. Unfortunately, in 1983, Moki was involved in a bicycle accident that left him paralyzed from the chest down. He had spent the past fifteen years in a wheelchair.

The large indoor hangar where the ceremony was taking place was decorated with red, white, and blue bunting, the Stars and Stripes and Hawaii state flags were positioned behind the podium, and over two hundred visitors and SEALs were in attendance. Rows and rows of chairs were arrayed in front of the podium, and the SEALs and sailors were all in tight formation at the back of the hangar.

After the usual pomp and circumstance, I approached the podium to give my remarks. When I concluded, Moki rolled himself up to the microphone, which we had positioned so that he could speak while seated in his wheelchair.

As Moki began to talk, it was apparent that the organizers had not positioned the microphone correctly. Even the front row could not hear Moki's remarks. I realized that I would have to get up from my chair, cross in front of the other dignitaries, and awkwardly reposition the microphone. Moki was just beginning to thank people, but if I didn't act soon, the audience would miss his inspirational comments.

As I started to rise from my chair, a young SEAL dressed in his white uniform broke ranks with the formation and marched past the two hundred attendees, directly up to the microphone. He came to attention, saluted Lieutenant Commander Martin, adjusted the microphone, saluted again, did an about-face, and returned to the formation. Not a single moment of Moki's talk was lost.

After the dedication was over, I approached the young SEAL and thanked him for his prompt action. He responded to me, "Sir, something had to be done and no one else was doing it. So I thought it was up to me." It may have been the best response to real leadership that I ever heard. "No one else was doing it, so it was up to me." It was the essence of Sua Sponte.

Real leadership is not *always* about being the person in charge during an existential crisis. You don't have to be Ralph Puckett, running across an open field while the enemy is trying to gun you down. Sometimes real leadership is just doing the right thing when no one else is. When you take action of your own accord, it sets the tone for the organization. It tells others that initiative is expected in the company and hopefully rewarded. It gives the employees a sense of empowerment. It gives them a sense of ownership. They will make mistakes and their mistakes will have repercussions, but...I guarantee you the mistakes of action are far less consequential than the mistakes of inaction.

It's Simple:

1. Foster a culture of action, allowing the rank and file to take the initiative and fix problems that need addressing.
2. Accept the fact that this will lead to zealousness and the occasional screwup. This overenthusiasm is better than a culture of inaction.
3. Praise those who attempt to solve problems on their own, even if the results are not as expected.

CHAPTER EIGHT

Who Dares Wins

It is better to err on the side of daring than the side of caution.

—ALVIN TOFFLER, AMERICAN WRITER AND FUTURIST

I looked at my watch. Thirty minutes until launch time. The bright orange can of Rip It energy drink on my desk was just about empty. I took one final sip, got up, and walked into the Tactical Operation Center. The TOC was a small windowless room filled with large flat-panel displays glowing with information about the evening's mission. Twenty people sat at their desks, glaring into their computer screens and coordinating last-minute instructions. The room was abuzz with activity, but very little noise. No one even noticed that I had entered the operations center. That was good. They needed to be focused. Tonight would be the biggest mission of their lives. If we got it wrong, we would bear the burden of failure for the rest of our days. If we got it right, it would be a legacy to be proud of.

We had to get it right.

"Alright, Chris. Time to go," I said.

Chris Faris, my command sergeant major and the senior enlisted man in the organization, was leaning over the shoulder of one of the intelligence analysts. He nodded to the young man, smiled, patted him on the back, and joined me at the door.

"Damn, these guys are good," Faris said.

"Well, they better be," I responded. "A lot is riding on them."

Faris and I walked out of the stuffy one-story concrete building and into the night air. Afghanistan after dark has a distinct smell. The air is both crisp and clean as the breezes come off the mountains and into the valleys below. And yet, there is a distinct odor of human life—smoke and sweat and dirt and wood—that cuts through nature's purity and enlivens your senses.

Our base at Jalalabad was surrounded by life. Thousands of Afghans lived in the nearby city, cooking their meals, tending their livestock, and caring for their families. To them, May 1, 2011, was just another night. But to those of us who were part of Operation Neptune's Spear, it was the night we hoped to get Osama bin Laden.

I checked my watch again. Twenty minutes until launch time.

Faris and I walked from the TOC, across a courtyard dotted with short, squatty palm trees, down a broken concrete sidewalk, and into an open area where the SEALs were making final preparations before heading to the helos. A fire burned brightly in the fire pit, and music was blaring from a nearby boom box. As I approached the gathering of heavily armed men, the master chief of the SEAL squadron turned off the music and yelled for everyone to gather around.

There was no tension in the air, just serious men getting ready to conduct a serious mission. A mission they all knew, victory or failure, would define them forever.

The SEALs grew quiet, looking at me. I motioned to Faris to say a few words. Faris had been in combat since he was eighteen years old. He understood, better than I, the mindset of the men getting ready to board the helicopters. Everyone in the formation knew Chris's background. He had received the Silver Star for heroism during the infamous Black Hawk Down incident. He had served in Bosnia. And for the past ten years, he had fought with an elite Army special operations force in Iraq. He had earned the SEALs' respect and they listened intently.

Even though it was May, the temperature in Jalalabad was cool enough to warrant a fire. Faris stepped up to the fire pit and rested his boot on one of the outside rocks.

Medium built, with black wavy hair, a square jaw, and dark penetrating eyes, Faris paused, looking at the twenty-four men who assembled around him. He glanced briefly down at the ground as if to gather his thoughts.

"Gentlemen, our British colleagues have a saying." He paused again, slowly looking from one end of the semicircle to the other. "Who Dares Wins. Tonight you will be daring greatly, and I know you will come out victorious."

Who Dares Wins. Three words that sum up the spirit of every great commando unit, and three words that differentiate a great leader from an average one.

In 1942, a lanky young British officer named David Stirling convinced his superiors that a small group of commandos could raid Field Marshal Erwin Rommel's panzer forces in North Africa with devastating effect. Stirling called his commandos the Special Air Service (SAS) in order to hide their real mission. After several unsuccessful attempts by ground and parachute, Stirling commandeered eighteen jeeps, mounted them with machine guns, and began jeep-borne attacks on the German fuel depots and airfields. Throughout 1942, Sterling personally led hit-and-run raids behind German lines. Rommel called Stirling the Phantom Major, owing to his ability to get behind German lines and get out undetected. Sterling was eventually captured, escaped, and was captured again, but his SAS commandos would go on to gain legendary status in North Africa. When asked to develop a motto for the SAS, Sterling chose the Latin phrase *Qui audet adipiscitur*: Who Dares Wins.

Just the day before the bin Laden mission launched, President Barack Obama had called me at my headquarters in Bagram, Afghanistan, to wish me and the SEALs good luck. I appreciated his call more than he could know, because I understood the immense pressure he was under. For the past seven months, the intelligence community had worked to determine whether the tall man who paced around the inside of the compound in Abbottabad, Pakistan, was bin Laden. But even with all the resources at our disposal, there was no way of verifying with certainty that "the Pacer" was the mastermind of 9/11. This meant that the president of the United States was going to have to make a decision on insufficient intelligence: a decision to send twenty-four SEALs and four helicopters into a sovereign country, onto a compound that was three miles from the Pakistani West Point, three miles from a major infantry battalion, and a mile from a police station. If the decision was wrong and the man who paced around the compound was nothing but a tall Pakistani, it would be the end of Obama's political career. He would bear the burden of the mission's failure for the rest of his life. Not to mention the possibility that lives on both sides could be lost on the mission. It was an enormous risk, but one the president knew he had to take. I admired his guts— *Who Dares Wins*—but more importantly, I admired his intellect for understanding the nature of the risks he was assuming.

Owing to the countless books and movies about Navy SEALs, there is a mistaken belief that when given a mission, we just grab our guns and go. The movies don't have time in the script to show all the planning and preparation that go into an operation. No one would read the books if half the chapters were about the military planning process. The readers, the audience, they want action. They want to see the derring-do, the heroics, the incredible drama that unfolds in combat. But who wants to see a bunch of guys with colored markers and whiteboards sketching out a detailed plan of action?

Daring greatly does not mean taking unnecessary risks. Any fool can be cavalier with the lives, the money, the future of others, either in business or combat. Daring greatly does mean having the boldness to push the envelope, to take advantage of an opportunity where others would recoil at the peril. But a great leader knows that they must reduce the risk to a manageable level, a level that is commensurate with the training or the talent of those executing the task.

In the three weeks leading up to the bin Laden raid, the Team spent 75 percent of their time planning the mission. We had extensive intelligence on the Pakistani integrated air defenses, the police, the military, the terrain, the weather, and bin Laden's compound. The plan we devised had 165 phases, in which we identified every training requirement, every piece of equipment needed, every intelligence shortfall, and every possible contingency. We tried to leave nothing to chance, even though we understood that chance and uncertainty are part of every mission. Where we couldn't properly assess the risk because the intelligence was incomplete (was bin Laden's compound booby-trapped, did he have an escape route underground?), we developed plans to deal with each contingency.

At one point in the mission, the lead MH-60 Black Hawk helicopter crashed in bin Laden's compound when the downblast from the blades created a vortex (a vacuum) over the helicopter and it lost lift. But owing to the extensive planning we had conducted, there was a backup helicopter not far behind. A downed helicopter was a calculated risk that we had anticipated and were prepared for.

After the mission was completed and bin Laden's remains were buried at sea, the world woke up to a jubilant America. Justice had been served. The president was rightfully applauded for his boldness, his willingness to take a risk on uncertain intelligence. When pressed about his decision, the president remarked that while the confidence level on bin Laden being in the compound was only 50 percent, he had 100 percent confidence in the SEALs, helo crews, and intelligence professionals who were conducting the mission. The president's decision to go was as analytical as it was bold.

When we look across history at the great risk-takers in business, entertainment, sports, the arts, or the military, we see that each of these men and women understood that in every risk there is an opportunity. The opportunity exists because the risks seemed too high, and others—those without the confidence to move forward—were too fearful to venture into a particular space. And yet, for every successful man and woman there are ten thousand failures. What separates the successes from the failures?

In 1991, I was a student at the Naval Postgraduate School in Monterey, California. For two years I worked on developing a theory of special operations. I wanted to know why special operations missions succeeded in spite of the fact that they were exceptionally high-risk. Was their boldness alone enough to carry the day? Were their commandos so superior to the enemy that they were bound to win in a fight? Was their technology so exceptional that it gave them an overwhelming advantage? As it turned out, those factors were necessary but certainly not sufficient for success. In each case, *Who Dares Wins* had to be backed up by *Who Plans and Prepares Wins*. It was only through extensive planning and preparation that the special operations leaders were able to identify the major risk factors and develop options for addressing them. To those on the outside looking in, the risks appeared great. However, to those on the inside, the risks were manageable.

Every great leader must exhibit a sense of boldness, because the rank and file don't want to follow a timid soul. Those leaders must be prepared to act when others are weak-kneed and fearful of failure. They must embrace the motto *Who Dares Wins*. But no leader should confuse daring and audacity with brashness and impudence. The former is fine, the latter will surely result in failure.

It's Simple:

1. Seek opportunities to take risks. No great leader was ever timid or weak-kneed.
2. Mitigate the risk through extensive planning and preparation.
3. Learn from your mistakes and be prepared to take the next big risk. Don't let a single failure define you.

CHAPTER NINE

Hope Is Not a Strategy

Setting a goal is not the main thing. It is deciding how you will go about achieving it and staying with that plan.

—COACH TOM LANDRY

The large video screen was propped awkwardly against the wall, yet to be bolted into the concrete. On the screen, divided into Hollywood Squares, were several senior officers from around the Washington counterterrorism community. In the room with me was my boss, General Stan McChrystal, the head of the special operations unit he commanded. It was February 2004, and McChrystal and I had stopped off in Doha, Qatar, to have a video call with our colleagues across the interagency.

Staring intently into the video screen, McChrystal said, "We intend to build a network of special operations and intelligence operators across the globe in order to counter the network being created by al Qaeda."

He paused.

"We need a network to defeat a network," McChrystal emphasized, more forcefully now.

"That's a pretty tall order," came one reply.

"I don't know if I can get our department to agree to this," another responded.

"Where are you going to get all these people from?" asked the representative from the Pentagon.

"I don't know, Stan," said one man, shaking his head.

McChrystal gathered his thoughts.

"Well, not only do we intend to build a network around the globe, but we also need each of you to provide us your best people so we can create an interagency task force."

I watched quietly as several people on the screen rolled their eyes and scratched their heads.

"Look, Stan, I appreciate what you're trying to do. It's a great vision," one of the more senior men commented, "but I'm not sure how you're going to pull this off."

The other folks around the video nodded in agreement.

"Well, we're all behind you," the senior man said without a lot of conviction. "And we're hoping for the best."

We're *hoping* for the best. We're *hoping* for the best.

As the video pictures faded, McChrystal got up from his chair, picked up a dry erase marker, went to the whiteboard, and together we began to map out a plan. *Hope* was not going to be our strategy.

There is some debate over the origin of the quote *Hope*

Is Not a Strategy. I first heard it when I was a young SEAL lieutenant in 1985. I made the mistake of telling my boss that after all our planning and training, I hoped the mission would go well. He quickly pounced on me and said that if hope was my strategy, the mission would likely fail. He sent me back to the planning room to ensure I had addressed *all* the risk factors. Some have attributed the quote to Vince Lombardi. The coach was the quintessential taskmaster and left nothing to chance when building his game plans for the Green Bay Packers. In 2001, there was a best-selling book by Rick Page entitled *Hope Is Not a Strategy: The 6 Keys to Winning the Complex Sale.* It was a business book, but the implication for any leader with a vision was the same: You must put in the hard work of turning the vision into a plan. A plan that had milestones and measurables, and produced results. For McChrystal, hope was important for our success because it inspired the troops to action, but hope without proper planning was just dreaming.

For the next several days, McChrystal, with the help of his staff, built the framework for a network. We knew where al Qaeda was operating from. We knew their logistics nodes, their travel routes, their financial hubs, their recruiting stations; now we had to put a person in every agency, every embassy, every allied military, every point of intersection where the terrorist organization had a presence. The information would be gathered and forwarded to our own Joint Interagency Task Force (JIATF), a collection of the best and brightest special operators, intelligence specialists, and law enforcement professionals we could gather.

Over the course of the following five years, Stan McChrystal built one of the most effective military organizations in the history of war fighting. The special operations network that Stan McChrystal created, along with his officers and NCOs, permeated every major institution of U.S. government and most of our counterterrorism allies. It is not hyperbole to say that McChrystal's force saved the lives of thousands of Americans and our friends; terrorist plots were disrupted, pirates were thwarted, dictators were displaced, evil men were put behind bars, all because Stan McChrystal and his team didn't rely on hope as a strategy.

———

It seems self-evident that a leader must have a vision, develop a strategy, and put a plan in place to bring the vision to reality. The concept is simple, but the execution is extremely difficult. It is difficult because it requires a leader's full attention, and with all leaders, there are a hundred things a day that divert your attention. I found during my times in command that a leader can only accomplish two or three major tasks during their tenure. If you stretch your attention too widely, nothing great gets done, because only you can keep the rank and file focused on the big tasks. Only you, the leader, can ensure that the manpower, the resources, the finances, and the energy are there to tackle the big jobs.

Never underestimate the power of hope. Hope is what inspires, hope is what encourages, hope is what empowers, and without hope, nothing worthwhile can be accomplished. But hope alone is just wishful thinking. Pair hope with a sound strategy, a detailed plan, and a lot of hard work, and nothing is out of reach.

It's Simple:

1. Have a vision that says *what* you are going to do. Make it bold and inspiring.
2. Have a strategy that tells *how* you are going to do it. Make it clear and concise.
3. Have a plan that shows *who* is responsible and the details of implementation. They must all be connected.

CHAPTER TEN

*No Plan Survives First Contact
with the Enemy*

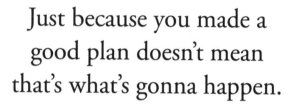

Just because you made a
good plan doesn't mean
that's what's gonna happen.

—TAYLOR SWIFT

D r. Russ Stolfi paced the floor in front of the pull-down screen, stopping occasionally to change the viewgraph on the overhead projector. In his early sixties, Stolfi was tall, clean-shaven, with a receding hairline and a penchant for military apparel that bordered on the eccentric. An expert on European warfare, Stolfi taught military history at the Naval Postgraduate School in Monterey, California.

Attired in a green camouflage dress suit, he was lecturing the class of military officers on one of his favorite subjects: Prussian general Helmuth von Moltke the Elder. Not to be confused, Stolfi bellowed, with Moltke's nephew, Helmuth von Moltke the Younger. Moltke the Elder was the Prussian Army's chief of staff for over thirty years. Widely considered to be one of the most brilliant military strategists in history, Moltke revitalized and modernized the Prussian military. In keeping with the thinking of fellow Prussian general Carl von Clausewitz, Moltke emphasized concentrating an army's mass and maneuvering to destroy his enemies.

Equally important, he realized that for modern armies to be successful, generals had to relinquish some of their control and put more authority and judgment into the hands of their subordinates. Having just returned from Operation Desert Storm, I found the discussion on Prussian military strategy both fascinating and still relevant in the 1990s.

Stolfi turned on the lights and shut off the overhead projector.

"Well, Commander McRaven," he said with some theatrics, "what is the most important lesson you have learned today?"

I quickly thought through the bullets Stolfi had greasepenciled on the viewgraph. They were all axioms of military strategy and tactics: War is a continuation of policy by other means; everlasting peace is a dream; to secure peace one must prepare for war; the fate of every nation rests in its power." I needed to pick one.

"War is a continuation of policy," I started.

"Oh please, Commander," Stolfi said, tapping his wooden pointer on my desk.

"What do you need to know as an officer? What is the most important thing you should consider when developing a plan? What is the most fundamental aspect of war strategy, operations, or tactics?"

Stolfi reached for his last viewgraph, turned off the lights, and before I could answer, he read the quote from Moltke the Elder.

It said, *"No plan of operations reaches with any certainty beyond the first encounter of the enemy's main force."*

"In other words," Stolfi said, "always have a *Plan B*. A contingency plan. A backup plan. Because once you encounter the enemy, no plan survives first contact."

Over the course of the next two years, with Dr. Russel Stolfi as my faculty advisor, I wrote my postgraduate thesis, entitled *The Theory of Special Operations*. As I researched ten famous missions in special operations history, it was clear to me that Moltke's old axiom stood the test of time. It was not something I would soon forget.

———

We were two minutes out. From the overhead video, I could see the twin Black Hawk helicopters screaming across the Pakistani landscape, side doors open, Navy SEALs poised to fast-rope into the Abbottabad compound that housed the most wanted man in the world, al Qaeda leader Osama bin Laden.

Inside my Afghanistan command center, I watched

intently as the first helo crested the eighteen-foot-high concrete wall and came to a hover just beside the three-story building housing bin Laden. As the pilot flared, ready to drop the fast rope, I could see the helo begin to waffle. The nose pitched upward and the tail swayed awkwardly from right to left. Over the radio I could hear the pilot struggling to gain control. Something was definitely wrong. Seconds later, the helo jerked violently forward, the tail swung wildly to the left, and the machine and men came crashing down into the outer courtyard, away from the planned landing spot.

The pilot of the second helo, seeing the hard landing of the lead helicopter, banked quickly to the right and landed his SEALs outside the compound. Everything we had initially planned had gone south. Now the SEALs from the first helo were isolated in another area of the compound, unable to quickly get to their objectives. The SEALs from the second helo, who were supposed to be on the roof of the three-story building, were outside the compound, having to breach their way through several metal doors just to get back. Watching from inside the White House, the president and his staff were holding their collective breaths. At that moment, it seemed as if the success of the operation hung in the balance. But as dire as the situation may have appeared, I knew we had a plan to get the mission back on track.

For three weeks prior to Operation Neptune's Spear, the mission to get Osama bin Laden, the SEALs and helicopter planners went over every contingency possible, expecting that things might go wrong. Not only had the planners anticipated having to deviate from their insertion point, but they had also anticipated that we might need a backup helo just in case one or both aircraft went down.

As planning would have it, the SEALs adjusted quickly and made their way into the compound. Within minutes they had reached the third floor and killed bin Laden. At the same time, the air component commander moved the backup helo into position, just in time to extract the SEALs and destroy the damaged Black Hawk. Within two hours, all the men were safely back in Afghanistan. Plan A had failed, but Plan B and Plan C were executed to perfection.

———

The Military Decision-Making Process (MDMP) is the fundamental tool officers and enlisted use when developing a plan of action for a military operation. It consists of a seven-step process that includes: receipt of the mission, mission analysis, course of action (COA) development, COA comparison, COA approval, and orders production and dissemination. There are a lot of variations on this process. The Marines use the Rapid Response Planning Process (R2P2). The Air Force and others use the Joint Planning System. And of course, most major companies have various stress tests they use to determine their preparedness to handle financial crises; tests like Monte Carlo, Dodd-Frank Act Stress Test (DFAST), or the Comprehensive Capital Analysis and Review (CCAR). However, all of them essentially require the planner to review the plan, develop options, test those options against the worst-case scenario, and ensure they have all the personnel, training, and equipment necessary to execute those options. Although not inherently part of the planning process, it's understood that you must rehearse the options to flesh out the potential areas of highest risk—and then refine the plan to reduce the risk as much as possible.

The problem with the MDMP or Monte Carlo or DFAST is that they are time and staff intensive. Additionally, if you begin with the wrong assumptions, you can come away with a false sense of security that you have addressed all the risk concerns. But, those concerns aside, if the mission or the problem you have as a company is truly important, then you need to invest the effort.

After the *Exxon Valdez* maritime disaster in 1989, the National Transportation Safety Board reported that the contingency planning performed by the Alyeska Pipeline, Exxon, and federal and state officials was inadequate. They concluded that many observers "focus on the low probability [of the event] and *assure* themselves that the high consequence event will never happen and that untested response plans will be adequate if it does." This approach to Plan B is often a fatal mistake.

As a leader, always ensure that your organization has put forth the effort to plan for the worst-case scenario even if it seems the least likely to happen, because Moltke the Elder was right: No plan survives first contact with the enemy. Always be ready.

It's Simple:

1. Always consider the worst-case scenario and plan accordingly.
2. Test the plan to ensure everyone in the organization knows how to react when things go poorly.
3. Be prepared. Murphy was an optimist.

CHAPTER ELEVEN

It Pays to Be a Winner

You have competition every day because you set such high standards for yourself that you have to go out every day and live up to that.

—MICHAEL JORDAN

I was struggling. The California sun was beating down on me, the summer wind from offshore was bearing against me, the sand along the beach was soft, and each stride in my jungle boots took more effort than I could muster. To make matters worse, the day before I had endured an additional two hours of calisthenics at the hands of the SEAL instructors. The infamous "Circus" was taking its toll.

"Come on, Mr. Mac! You're an officer," the chief shouted. "You shouldn't be at the back of the pack. Pick it up!"

The instructor, dressed in a blue-and-gold T-shirt, khaki shorts, and green jungle boots, seemed to glide effortlessly across the sand, not a drop of sweat beading on his forehead. How was that possible? I wondered.

Ahead of me was a long line of SEAL trainees, strung out over a hundred yards. Minutes earlier we had hit the turnaround point of a four-mile beach run, and now everyone was picking up the pace for the final push to the end. Everyone but me. I was Tail-End Charlie. The anchorman.

The last guy in the line, and I was barely able to hold that position!

The instructor, a highly decorated Vietnam SEAL with the lean body of a distance runner, pulled up beside me and whispered in my ear.

"You're better than this, Mr. Mac. I know you are."

He was right. I was a high school and college miler and one of the better runners in the class. But now I was exhausted from days of hard training. My tank was empty. At this point there wasn't anything that could motivate me to move faster. And then he said it.

"Remember, Mr. Mac. It pays to be a winner!"

It pays to be a winner. It pays to be a winner. The saying was used by every instructor in SEAL training. The expectation was that SEALs were winners. And the only way to be a winner was to set the bar high. High standards of fitness. High standards of professionalism. High standards of conduct. Winners worked hard. Winners sacrificed. Winners never quit. If you were going to be a SEAL, you had to be a winner—that's why we had all volunteered to undergo training. We wanted to be winners.

While the saying was designed to inspire you to action, there was also an implied threat that if you didn't meet the standard, there would be a price to pay. On the beach runs, that price was the "Goon Squad." Everyone who failed to cross the finish line in the prescribed time, who failed to meet the high standard of physical fitness, would immediately be rounded up and sent on another one-mile run. Failing that event, the remaining trainees would get another one-mile run. And then of course, a failed event would lead to a Circus after the end of the day's activities.

I began to pump my arms faster. My legs churned a little quicker. I dug deep and took off. One by one I passed my fellow trainees. I could see in the distance the lead runner. Ensign Fred Artho. Artho was a marvel of human engineering. He was the fittest man in the class and had no sense of pain. He could run forever and smile through it all.

The instructor was matching my pace.

"Faster, faster," he yelled.

We were now at the Coronado jetty. Only one mile left. Out of the corner of my eye I could see the blue-and-gold T-shirt of the instructor. Now he was sweating but smiling at my effort.

The Coronado Shores, a condominium complex of four buildings that paralleled the beach, were passing by one by one. There was only a quarter mile left.

"Dig, dig, dig," I yelled at myself.

"Now!" the instructor screamed. "Push it, push it!"

My lungs were burning, my legs numb from the adrenaline, and my eyes coated in sand and sweat.

Three runners in front of me. Only three.

With my last ounce of effort, I drove my legs as hard as I could, lunging toward the finish line.

Tumbling into the sand, I crossed in third place.

"Not bad, Mr. Mac. Not bad." The instructor smiled, catching his breath.

As I graduated from SEAL training and went on in the Teams, the saying *It Pays to Be a Winner* faded from the lexicon of the younger SEALs. Only us old guys remembered this incessant chant by the instructors. But what didn't fade was the importance of high standards and the expectation that if you were the best, your standards were high.

In July of 1990, I was the task unit commander for a SEAL detachment on a deployment to the Western Pacific. As part of the task unit, I had a boat detachment of two SEAFOX high-speed craft, a communications element, and a SEAL platoon. After thirty days of sailing across the Pacific, the five-ship Amphibious Ready Group, of which we were part, pulled into Subic Bay, Philippines. Within hours of docking, the two thousand embarked Marines and twenty-one SEALs were allowed to go ashore on liberty. The next morning, I received word that one of my SEALs had gotten into a bar fight and things had turned nasty. As it happened, that same night twenty-two Marines had gotten into an equal amount of trouble.

At 0800 I heard my name broadcast across the ship's intercom.

"Commander McRaven, report to the bridge."

This was not a good sign. I knew that the commodore, my boss, would be waiting to grill me.

As I made my way from the berthing area, up three flights of ladders to the bridge, I started to prepare my defense. Yes, my SEAL had gotten into trouble, but how did that compare to the twenty-two Marines who were equally egregious?

Entering the bridge, I found Mike Coumatos, the commodore, sitting in his captain's chair. I approached the chair and came to a modified attention.

"Sir, you called for me."

Coumatos got down from the chair and I could see the anger on his face. A Vietnam-era helo pilot, he was tactically brilliant, and over the course of the past eighteen months I had come to deeply respect him for his leadership of the Amphibious Ready Group. To this day, I count

Mike Coumatos as one of the finest leaders with whom I ever served.

Only five foot five, he closed the distance between us and glared up at me, just inches from my face.

"One of your SEALs got into a bar fight last night and beat up a couple of Marines. This is entirely unacceptable!"

"Yes sir, I completely agree," I started. And then I made a fatal mistake.

"But sir, I would also note that twenty-two Marines got in trouble last night."

Before I could continue, Coumatos moved toe to toe, his face now fully flushed with anger.

"They're young Marines, Bill," he said. "I expect them to get into trouble."

And then I was reminded why I was a Navy SEAL.

"But I hold you and your SEALs to a higher standard. And I expect you, as their leader, to do the same. Are we clear?"

I hold you and your SEALs to a higher standard. Those words resonated in my head for the rest of my career. While as a SEAL organization we have occasionally failed to meet those high standards (and dealt with the painful and embarrassing aftermath), we have never stopped raising the bar and trying to be the best. And I have always known that as a leader in this community my job was to ensure the standards of conduct and professionalism were met. Which meant not only establishing the standards but holding people accountable.

What you learn about high standards is how important they are to any organization. No one looks around and says, "Where is that mediocre team? That's what I want to be part of—a mediocre team." I don't care whether you are flipping hamburgers, washing cars, playing sports, or in the military. Everyone wants to be part of something special. Everyone wants to be a valued member of a great organization. And the only way to be a great organization is to set high standards and expect people to live up to those standards.

As leaders we sometimes struggle by placing unreasonable expectations on the men and women who serve with us. We are quick to understand the challenges of setting the bar too high. However, I will tell you that the young men and women who work for you long to be challenged, they seek to be the best, they want to be winners, and sometimes that means paying the price of hard work, high standards, and accountability. Never underestimate the value of a stretch goal, of setting the bar high and challenging your employees to clear it.

It's Simple:

1. Establish a winning culture by setting high standards. Your employees want to be challenged.
2. Hold people accountable when they fail to meet the standards. Accountability is the only thing separating the high performers from the pack.
3. Acknowledge those who meet or exceed the standard. It will reinforce the winning culture.

CHAPTER TWELVE

A Shepherd Should Smell Like His Sheep

From this day to the
ending of the world,
But we in it shall be
remembered;
We few, we happy few,
we band of brothers;
For he today that sheds his
blood with me
Shall be my brother.

—WILLIAM SHAKESPEARE,
HENRY V

With a long green seabag slung over my shoulder and only the glow of a small red light to guide me, I felt my way into the crew's berthing area, arm extended, eyes squinted, head moving from side to side. It was almost midnight and the Navy ensign who had picked me up at the Hickam Air Force Base in Hawaii told me that crew muster aboard the USS *Ouellet* was at 0630 the next morning.

It was June of 1974, and as a midshipman third class, I was on my summer cruise, a seven-week deployment to Pearl Harbor, Hawaii. As a junior midshipman, I would be berthed with the sailors, eat with the sailors, and work with the sailors. For the next seven weeks I would be an enlisted man learning everything I could from the sailors aboard the ship. The experience would forever change my approach to leadership.

Slipping off my shoes, I started to climb into my rack,

which was situated at the top of a stack of three other bunks. Gently I placed my foot on the metal railing of the first rack and eased myself upward. Grabbing the nylon straps of the top bunk, I started to pull myself up, when my foot slipped, and instinctively I lunged for another foothold. I knew immediately my foot had found flesh. A deep roar came from the rack below mine, and out rolled one of the biggest men I had ever seen in my young nineteen years.

"What the hell, bro! What the hell!" he yelled.

As I clung to the side of the stack of racks, a massive Samoan giant emerged with arms as big as my thighs and a face seething with anger, the red light of the berthing area flashing off his eyes.

"Hey man, I'm really sorry," I said, trying to climb down from the rack.

"Shut the hell up! I'm trying to sleep here," someone bellowed from a distant rack.

Rubbing his offended face with one hand, the Samoan grabbed me by the shirt and pulled me in close.

"Who the hell are you, bro?" he shouted, unconcerned about the rest of the sleeping sailors.

"Pipe down!" came another voice.

"Bill McRaven—I'm a midshipman—just got in an hour

ago—I was given the top rack—hey man, I'm really sorry about stepping on your face." I tried to get everything into one long sentence in case it was my last.

The giant Samoan turned me to one side, gazed for a moment, and then turned me the other way.

"You know, bro, this face of mine is the only one I got. And it's pretty and I don't want no one messin' it up. The ladies like it this way."

"Yeah, yeah, you bet."

He let go of my shirt and grabbed my seabag.

"This yours?" he asked.

"Yeah."

"Come on, bro, let's stow it in the bosun's locker for tonight and you can get it in the morning."

After stowing my seabag, I climbed into my rack fully clothed as he waited until I was safely out of his way.

"By the way, bro, my name's Ricky. Welcome to the Navy. Now get some sleep, bro. Quarters come early."

Over the course of the next seven weeks, Ricky took me under his wing and taught me everything he knew about being a sailor. There were the mundane lessons—like the fact that if you hold the power buffer too tightly you will lose control. Or the best way to press your dungarees is to put them under your mattress at night. Or it takes a good toothbrush and baking soda to get the stains off a urinal. And, of course, I learned where every good bar, dice game, and pawnshop were in Honolulu. Ricky was particularly good with the dice.

Knowing these tips and tricks served me well in building a relationship with my sailors, but I also learned the truly important lessons. I learned that every sailor had a story. A story about why they joined the Navy. A story about their family. A story about their hometown. And more than anything else, they had a story about their overseas deployments: the storm that almost capsized the ship; their near-death experience during an underway replenishment; the beautiful Polynesian princess they almost married; the card game where they took the entire pot; the dragon tattoo and how it got on their rear end; their crossing-the-equator ceremony; and the amazing sunsets at sea. Not only did every sailor have a story, but they all wanted to tell their stories and they all wanted you to listen. You can learn a lot by listening to the people you work with.

I also learned that sailors like Ricky wanted to be part of something special. They took pride in their ship, and while they would complain incessantly about the chow, the long hours, the officers, and the other crewmen, they would defend the reputation of their ship to anyone who was not part of the crew.

Knowing I would someday be wearing ensign bars, Ricky and his other crewmates made sure I understood what they expected from their officers.

"That dude," Ricky said, referring to a young lieutenant, "he shows up every day and spends an hour in the boiler room with me. Now that's a good officer, bro!

"The XO, he's a hard-ass when he has to be, but cuts us some slack when he can. He's good too.

"The skipper rides us hard, but he always makes sure we get the best spot on the pier."

The officers they respected the most were the ones who showed up in the boiler room when it was 120 degrees, who got greasy and turned wrenches with them, who picked up a broom to help with evening sweep-down, who brought them water when they were painting the side of the ship, and who thanked them routinely for their efforts. But they also wanted an officer who made the tough decisions, held them accountable, worked hard, and above all they wanted an officer who valued them for the tough work they did. Finally, they wanted an officer they could be proud of—even if they didn't say it publicly. They wanted someone who was smart, athletic, looked good in their uniform, and didn't embarrass them on liberty by getting too drunk or too rowdy.

Three years later I was commissioned an ensign in the Navy and headed off to Basic Underwater Demolition/ SEAL Training (BUD/S). The lessons from my time with Ricky were never far from my mind—share the misery, share the dangers, share the camaraderie, listen to their stories and you will learn about your sailors, and you will learn what they expect from you.

SEAL training was unlike most other courses in the military. The officers and the enlisted men went through the exact same training—the same soft-sand runs, the same open-ocean swims, the same obstacle course, the same harassment, the same days of being cold, wet, and miserable. The same Hell Week. Sharing the hardships with our enlisted men gave the officers an understanding of what motivated the men, and it also gave the men a level of respect for their officers because they had shared a common bond.

Over the course of the next thirty-seven years, I tried to spend as much time in the field with my SEALs as possible. As I rose in rank, that task became harder, and sometimes I tried to convince myself that the work I was doing in the office was more important. Now, clearly, the strategic work of any organization is important, but knowing how your decisions affect the rank and file is equally important. If, as a leader, you fail to spend time on the factory floor, you fail to walk around the cubicles, you fail to talk to the interns, you fail to have coffee with the junior employees, then you will fail to understand what's happening in your business. And, as a leader, you will eventually just fail.

During my time in Iraq and Afghanistan, I watched the great generals (and the colonels, majors, captains, lieutenants, and senior enlisted personnel) and how they interacted with their troops. The good ones spent time at the front lines, dodging bullets in Fallujah, riding in a Humvee on Route Irish, flying in a helo over the Hindu Kush, or just talking to the soldiers who manned the watchtowers. This engagement was not only important to understanding the troops, and thereby making better decisions; it was also vitally important for the troops to see their leaders getting sweaty and dirty right beside them.

Pope Francis once said, "A shepherd should smell like his sheep." While it's a relatively new saying, it mirrors the thinking of all great leaders for all time. If you lose touch with the men and women who work for you, if you can't relate to them because you spend too much time in the office and not enough time on the factory floor, if you don't "smell" like the people you are sworn to protect and lead, then you will be a poor leader who makes bad decisions.

It's Simple:

1. Share the hardships with your employees. You will gain their respect and learn about yourself as a leader.
2. Share the camaraderie. Let the employees see you having fun (within reason). They want to know that their leader is human as well.
3. Listen to the rank and file. They have solutions to most of the problems you struggle with.

CHAPTER THIRTEEN

Troop the Line

★

If you make listening and observation your occupation, you will gain much more than you can by talk.

—ROBERT
BADEN-POWELL,
FOUNDER OF
THE BOY SCOUTS

"Trooping the line" is steeped in Army tradition. Historically, generals have ordered their soldiers to muster on the parade field so the officers could inspect the troops, ask questions about their training, and ensure the general's orders were being relayed to the youngest private in the formation. Washington, Grant, Pershing, Eisenhower, Colin Powell, and the Army's first four-star female general, Ann Dunwoody: All the great generals have at some point trooped the line.

Each service has something similar. In the Navy, every morning the sailors and Marines would gather on the fantail or the flight deck of the ship to receive the daily word. In the Air Force, the airmen muster on the flight line, and orders are disseminated. In all cases, there is a deep understanding that as an officer you need to get out among the troops. You need to confirm that the senior officer's orders are being followed, but you also need to ensure the troops see their leader as often as possible.

In every command tour I had, trooping the line—those daily walks around the building, the base, or the camp—always yielded great insights into how well the organization was doing and how well I was leading.

———

"You heading out, sir?" the colonel asked, looking up from his computer.

"Just going for a walk," I replied.

He glanced up at the digital clock perched high above the wall of flat-panel displays, and smiled. It was four a.m. Afghanistan time. Time for my evening ritual.

"The last mission should be completed within the hour, sir," he said. "If there are any problems, I'll track you down."

"Roger. Thanks."

The Joint Operations Center (JOC) at my headquarters in Bagram, Afghanistan, was unusually quiet for a Saturday morning. Three Rangers missions in Kandahar and Ghazni Province were already completed. The high-value targets the soldiers were seeking had been captured, but two Rangers had been wounded in one of the assaults. Fortunately, nothing serious. Outside Jalalabad in eastern

Afghanistan, a SEAL mission was still in progress. As I was leaving the JOC, I could see the Predator feed zoom in on the Afghan compound the SEALs were raiding. Tiny black silhouettes moved with purpose from building to building. Beams from their laser designators zipped across the screen as the SEALs swept through the open courtyard, looking for their target.

Just another night in Afghanistan.

As I started to leave the building, I noticed the young guard at the Entry Control Point (ECP) carefully and methodically arranging the access badges on the table in front of her. Many of the soldiers who supported my special operations force were on a one-year deployment, and owing to the classified nature of our missions, most had no clue as to who we were.

I stopped briefly to chat with her. She was new to the Army. From Ohio. Loved the Buckeyes. Had three brothers. Made her tough. One of her brothers joined the Marines. But he was still stateside. She was the first of her family to serve in the Army. First to go to war. She was proud. She was a bit scared. But people here were nice. She was glad to be serving with us. *By the way, who were we?*

I thanked her for enlisting. Told her the folks in Ohio would be proud of her. *I was proud of her*. She signed up knowing she was going to war and did it anyway. As for who we were, well, we were a special operations force hunting the most wanted men in Afghanistan. A big smile came across her face. Her brother would be jealous, she said. "Yes, he would," I answered.

Outside the two-story plywood building with its fluorescent lights, computer screens, drone feeds, and exit signs, the Afghan night was spectacularly dark. While there is always a dull yellow glow hovering over the airfield, once you ventured out, a flashlight was a necessity.

I turned right after leaving the ECP and walked slowly down the gravel road that was the main street on our camp. The five-acre facility in the middle of Bagram Air Base housed over a thousand people. While the base chow hall and hospital were outside our facility, everything else we needed to plan and prepare our missions was enclosed within the walled-in area.

In the next hour, I swung by the motor pool, where I found there was a shortage of mechanics. I passed by the laundromat, where half the machines didn't work, and now I was heading to the last stop on my walk—the guard towers.

Every fifty yards along the outer perimeter, there was a twenty-foot-tall structure with a metal lattice frame and a small six-by-six-foot building on the top. The tiny building had a gunport on all four sides, but the heavy caliber machine gun was pointing toward the open fields from where the Taliban would launch their assaults. In all the years I had been on Bagram, we had never had a ground assault that threatened the camp. Nevertheless, we were prepared if it came.

I climbed up the ladder leading to the trapdoor at the bottom of the tiny room. Knocking first, I slowly lifted the door, ensuring I didn't smash the soldier inside.

"You're clear," he said.

So as not to ruin the soldier's night vision, I turned off my headlamp and crawled into the room.

"How are you doing tonight?" I said, slowly standing up.

"Fine, dude. How are you?" the soldier responded, unable to tell who I was in the dark.

"Good, good," I responded. "I'm Admiral McRaven."

"Cool," he said, clearly unsure of what an admiral was or why an admiral would be in his watchtower at four a.m.

"Quiet tonight?" I asked.

"Oh, yeah. Just a bunch of kids throwing rocks from across the field. I don't think they like us."

"I think you might be right." I smiled in the dark.

"Three-four, this is . . ." the radio crackled.

"Station calling, this is three-four, say again your last," the soldier said, pulling the handheld walkie-talkie from his belt holder.

"I say again . . ." came the unintelligible response.

"Damn batteries are dying," the soldier complained. "I knew I should have checked them before coming on duty."

Glancing down at his watch, he pushed the night-light button and checked the time.

"It's just their routine check-in," he mumbled to himself.

Squeezing the push-to-talk button again, he shouted into the radio.

"This is three-four, all good here!"

Listening intently, I could make out the faint sound of a "Roger."

Private Joey Benson from Colorado turned out to be a talkative fellow. Old for a private, he hated the Army. But after a number of misdemeanor violations, the judge didn't give him much choice. It was jail or the Army. He was just riding out his time in the service and then wanted to go back to Colorado to ski. He hoped to stay out of further trouble. He hated the Army, he said again, but he loved his fellow soldiers. He hated the Army, but he actually enjoyed being in Afghanistan. He hated the Army, but his officers and NCOs were pretty cool. He hated the Army, but he was learning how to be a mechanic. He hated the Army, but man he loved to shoot. Yeah, he couldn't wait to get out of the Army, but it would be cool to be a sergeant. He could really teach these young kids how to be soldiers.

———

The next morning at 1100 hours Zulu time, we held our standard worldwide video conference. My special operations task force was arrayed across the globe in bases and camps large and small. We reviewed every major operation from Iraq to Afghanistan, from Somalia to North Africa, from the Philippines to Yemen. Every high-value target. Every existential threat to the nation. All the wildly important issues of the day. After an hour, I took to the microphone one last time. As usual, the officers and NCOs were eagerly waiting for some sage wisdom from the "old man," something deep and meaningful, something that would change the course of their fight against al Qaeda, the Taliban, Al-Shabaab, Boko Haram, and Abu Sayyaf.

"Folks, I did my walkaround last night and I discovered

a few things. I want each of you commanders and senior NCOs to address these important issues."

On the thirty video screens in front of me, I could see pens preparing to write down the next great commandments from on high.

"First, I want all the support soldiers briefed on who we are as a task force. I want them to be part of this team. I'm proud to have them and I want them to be proud to be here."

A few noses wrinkled, a few faces squinched. Briefing the conventional soldiers was considered a security risk—*but alright, old man, if that's what you want.*

"Next, I want every senior NCO to check their laundromats and ensure all the machines are working. If they're not, let my chief of staff know, and let's get new ones."

Laundromats? Are you kidding me? The three-star admiral is worried about laundromats? That's what junior NCOs are supposed to worry about.

"After that, I want the commanders to review the vehicle-to-mechanic ratio in your motor pools. We should have at least one mechanic for every three to four vehicles. If it's greater than that, then let my chief know and we will get you additional help."

Okay, fair enough. We all need more mechanics.

"Finally, I want each watchtower supervisor to do an individual inspection prior to every watch rotation. I want to ensure the watch standers have fresh batteries in their radios and all the training they need to properly fire the fifty-cal."

Man, we are really in the weeds now...

"Everybody good with that?" I said, asking the proverbial rhetorical question.

Half-hearted nods all around.

Every leader understands that nothing is more important to the success of a mission than the morale of the troops. But leaders often misunderstand the nature of morale. Morale is not just about the employees feeling *good*, it is about the employees feeling *valued*. It is about the rank and file having the resources they need to do their job. It is about the troops believing that their leader is listening to their concerns.

Within a few weeks all the washers and dryers worked, the motor pool was humming with new mechanics, and at 1:00 a.m. Afghanistan time on May 14, 2009, fourteen Taliban fighters crossed the open field in front of the camp, throwing grenades and firing on the towers. The guards in the watchtowers opened up with a synchronized response, helping to thwart the attack.

Trooping the line has always served me well, whether in

the military or as the chancellor of the University of Texas System. Leaders can often convince themselves that they are too important to be dealing with the mundane issues of the organization. They, *the true leaders*, are meant to be solving the intractable problems, the problems that will advance the organization to the next level, the problems that only the smartest men or women in the company can solve.

True, but...

Never forget that there are also problems that need solving at the lowest possible level. Problems that, if not addressed, result in inefficiency, ineffectiveness, and low morale. Problems that the lower echelons in the organization struggle to solve but that the leader can solve with one short directive. And sometimes the only way to ferret out these problems is to get out of your office and talk to the men and women who do the hard work on your behalf.

It's Simple:

1. Get out of your office and talk to the employees at the far end of the chain of command.
2. Find an opportunity to solve small but seemingly intractable problems.
3. Ensure your senior staff know that these "little problems" can have major effects on morale.

CHAPTER FOURTEEN

Expect What You Inspect

Truth is confirmed by inspection and delay; falsehood by haste and uncertainty.

—TACITUS,
ROMAN HISTORIAN

In 1778, the Continental Army under George Washington was floundering. Volunteers with no military training were called into action and were roundly defeated by the regulars of the British Army. With no discipline, no organizational structure, and frighteningly low morale, these farmers, tradesmen, and merchants struggled to conduct even the simplest of military maneuvers.

By the winter of that year, Washington had moved his forces to Valley Forge, outside Philadelphia. He desperately needed someone to help him build a professional army. Benjamin Franklin, who was in Europe at the time, found exactly the right man for the job.

Mounted on a large white horse, with full military regalia on his uniform and two immense pistols holstered at his side, General Friedrich Wilhelm von Steuben rode into Valley Forge in February of 1778. One soldier recalled von Steuben's arrival as though it was "the fabled God of War himself."

Von Steuben had been a soldier since the age of seventeen, fighting in the Seven Years' War, where he was wounded on several occasions. He had gone on to serve as a quartermaster, an adjutant, and the aide-de-camp to Frederick the Great. He was a soldier's soldier.

Soon after his arrival, Washington made von Steuben the Continental Army's inspector general. Von Steuben was appalled by what he saw of the volunteer army. The camp at Valley Forge was poorly laid out: Tents and huts were scattered across the field, the soldiers relieved themselves wherever they wanted, sanitation was nonexistent, and both weapons and equipment were in unacceptable working order. In addition, owing to a lack of good record-keeping, corruption and graft were rampant as soldiers received and then sold their muskets and other equipment.

Within days, von Steuben had initiated inspections of the troops, their tents, their rifles, and their combat equipment. Administrative records were also scrutinized to eliminate war profiteering. Soon thereafter, daily drills began, and during the winter of 1778, von Steuben wrote the *Regulations for the Order and Discipline of the Troops of the United States*—a document that has been the foundation for the American military since it was first published.

Baron von Steuben's influence on the Continental Army is credited with much of their success, and for the past 245 years the idea of good order and discipline and the value of inspections has been a mainstay of every great military organization. And no leader of any good standing has ever questioned the need for inspections.

———

Colonel Elliot "Bud" Sydnor walked along the shoulder of the road examining the three 18-wheelers lined up bumper to bumper, ready to move out. Inside the cabin of the tractor were heavily armed federal agents from the Office of Secure Transportation. Inside the fifty-three-foot-long trailer was sensitive material being shipped across country.

For the past three weeks, Sydnor, a retired Green Beret, had been training the new agents in protective detail procedures. Every conceivable threat to the convoy had been rehearsed: a terrorist ambush, an activist group roadblock, a vehicle breakdown. Every officer had specific responsibilities for each scenario. Nothing could be left to chance in moving this dangerous cargo. But training was over now, and this was a real mission.

Sydnor had relinquished oversight of the mission to the senior federal agent, a police captain. The agent was now in charge and would oversee the actual movement of the material. As Sydnor observed the final preparations for movement, one thing caught his attention: At no time had the captain conducted a personnel inspection of each guard on the truck.

He approached the agent and tactfully said, "I'm sorry, Captain, but I noticed that you didn't conduct a personnel inspection of your troops."

The captain, looking somewhat annoyed, rolled his eyes and said, "Well, Colonel, we're all professionals here. There's no need for an inspection."

Sydnor, a man of quiet disposition but with a penchant for detail, replied pointedly, "Well, Captain, if you were a real professional, you would understand the value of an inspection."

The captain paused, remembering the service of the man in front of him, and within minutes each agent was lined up as the captain went man by man to ensure all their equipment was in place and operational. The captain knew that if anybody understood the value of an inspection, it was Bud Sydnor.

Colonel Elliot "Bud" Sydnor was the ground force

commander for one of the most storied special operations in history, the raid on the POW camp in Son Tay, North Vietnam. On November 21, 1970, six helicopters carrying seventy soldiers, supported by four C-130 gunships and refuelers, flew from Thailand across Laos and into North Vietnam in an effort to rescue approximately sixty American POWs being held at Camp Hope near Son Tay. Additionally, there were hundreds of Navy and Air Force support aircraft and personnel involved in the mission. It was Sydnor who developed the training curriculum, conducted the rehearsals, oversaw the inspections, and led the force at the POW compound. During the mission, Sydnor's heroism would earn him the second-highest award for valor, the Distinguished Service Cross. When he retired after thirty-one years, his decorations also included the Silver Star, the Legion of Merit with two oak leaf clusters, the Distinguished Flying Cross, the Bronze Star, and countless other awards.

The Son Tay raid was one of the boldest, most complex operations in modern military history. Unfortunately, prior to the raid the North Vietnamese had moved the POWs because of tainted drinking water in their well. When the raid force arrived, they encountered stiff resistance from a heavily armed North Vietnamese company, and after a lengthy firefight they realized the POWs were gone. Even though no POWs were rescued, the organization and execution of the mission were flawless. Forty years later, I would use the Son Tay raid as the template for Operation Neptune's Spear, the mission to get bin Laden.

Every military in the world understands the significance of an inspection. We inspect uniforms, weapons, vehicles, tanks, airplanes, ships, and everything that is of value to the organization. But too often, in the corporate world, we give it less attention than we should. While every CEO appreciates the internal and external audits to verify the financial status of the company, that same rigor is not always applied to the other core elements of the firm. What is often lost is the positive effect that inspections can have on morale. Inspections are not just about ensuring compliance; inspections force a level of discipline into the corporate system, and when discipline is applied, the rank and file know they are in an organization that cares about quality, that cares about results, that cares about hard work. No one loves to be inspected. But every professional appreciates knowing that someone above them cares about the details, because it is in the details that businesses succeed or fail.

As a leader, you must find the right balance between

too much oversight and too little scrutiny. Left unattended, most organizations will get sloppy and undisciplined. It is human nature. Your employees must understand that their work will be judged, reviewed, inspected, and graded. It is the only way to ensure compliance with the high standards you set. While the troops will always complain about too much oversight and too many inspections, they will also appreciate knowing what's expected of them.

It's Simple:

1. Identify the core competencies within your organization.
2. Develop a plan to inspect these areas on a regularly scheduled basis.
3. Show up during an inspection to ensure the rank and file understand that you, the leader, value the process and their efforts.

CHAPTER FIFTEEN

Communicate, Communicate, Communicate

Effective teamwork begins and ends with communication.

—MIKE KRZYZEWSKI,
BASKETBALL COACH

S an Clemente Island is a rugged piece of terrain that rises out of the Pacific Ocean eighty miles west of San Diego. Approximately twenty-one miles long and four miles wide, it is often obscured by low-hanging fog and has that "Island of King Kong" look from afar. For the past sixty years, San Clemente has been the home of the Third Phase of Navy SEAL training. After almost six months of a grueling selection process, the few students who remain come to San Clemente hoping to complete the last three weeks of training.

This final phase is oftentimes the hardest. On the first night, the SEAL instructors take you three miles off the coast, drop you in the water, and tell you to swim back to shore. They also take great pleasure in briefing you about all the sharks that feed in the waters off San Clemente. Then there is the sixteen-mile run, the five-mile swim, the endless nights of demolition and weapons work, the daily physical training, and the constant harassment designed to break your spirit and test your mettle. Not only is San

Clemente the final proving ground for aspiring SEALs, it is also the most important test for the officers and senior enlisted. No other aspect of SEAL training places as much emphasis on leadership. Here on the island, you will lead your platoon through a series of trials: short combat drills designed to test your ability to command and control under the most difficult of circumstances. One of those trials is the Ambush Drill.

Our class, which had begun with 110 men six months ago, was now down to thirty-three. We were mentally tough, highly motivated, physically imposing, and way too cocky for our own good. That morning we had mustered on a small plateau on the northwest side of the island. A gray mist hung over the lower parts of the island and floated out into the choppy sea. From the shoreline, cliffs rose steeply in all directions. Most of the terrain on San Clemente was scrub brush, cactus, and rocks, but there was one piece of ground where the brush and the small trees created a tiny forest of vegetation—a forest thick enough to hide seven large men armed with assault rifles, machine guns, and grenade simulators. A forest long enough for another fourteen men to patrol down a path, waiting to be ambushed.

Chief Faketty paced in front of the assembled group of students.

"Alright, gentlemen, the drill today is simple. You will walk down the path we choose for you, and at some point, hiding in the heavy underbrush, will be the instructors. They will initiate the ambush with blank ammunition and grenade simulators, and you must negotiate your way out of the kill zone as quickly as possible. Is that clear?"

"Yes, Instructor Faketty," we all yelled simultaneously.

"Mr. Mac, grab your platoon. You will be going first," Faketty said.

I quickly assembled the other thirteen students and put them into patrol formation. At the front of the patrol was Seaman Dave LeBlanc, the point man. LeBlanc was the best map-and-compass guy in the class and the man with the keenest eyes and the sharpest ears. As the platoon commander, I fell in at the number two spot. Immediately behind me was the radioman. My position in the line of march allowed me to direct the point man and then turn around and, through the radioman, communicate with my artillery, air, or naval gunfire support. Back in those days there was only one radio per platoon. All our internal platoon communications were done by "hand and arm" signals or yelling loudly in the middle of a firefight. After the radioman were the heavy machine gunner, seven riflemen, a corpsman, another machine gunner, and then the rear security. All in all, a pretty significant amount of firepower for a small fourteen-man element.

Jim Varner, a petty officer first class, stepped forward from the group. An experienced fleet sailor, Varner was the most senior of the enlisted men in the class.

"Everyone needs to be paying attention to Mr. Mac," he said. "If he 'survives' the first volley of fire, he will tell us which way to move. The instructors will be throwing smoke and grenade simulators, so listen to the commands from Mr. Mac and watch for his hand and arm signals."

Marshall Lubin, the rear security, spoke up.

"And make sure you relay his commands down the line so I'm not left out in the cold!"

Everyone nodded. They knew the drill. If I said "Move forward," we ran forward. If I said "Move to the left," we moved to the left. In an ambush, the most important thing was to get out of the kill zone as quickly as possible. This required everyone to be on the same sheet of music. If the platoon commander wasn't communicating his intent, if the platoon didn't react as one body, if everyone wasn't firing in the same direction, then disaster was inevitable.

After one final check of our weapons and blank-firing adapters, we lined up and moved out. The fog had lifted on the coast, but a stiff breeze was whipping across the plateau. The tangy smell of salt water and the putrid stench of nesting sea lions filled my nostrils. Dressed in a solid-green utility uniform, a flop hat, canvas jungle boots, an H-harness for my ammo, and carrying my M16 rifle, I felt every bit a Navy SEAL.

After about fifteen minutes patrolling across the open plateau, we arrived at the dirt path that led into the underbrush. I motioned with my hand to signal that the enemy could be in the area. The signal was passed down the line. Not knowing where the attack would come from, I was listening for any sounds that weren't natural, and my eyes kept darting back and forth, left to right.

Every bush that moved caught my eye. Every twig that snapped turned my head. Every shadow cast from the moving sun made me see men that weren't there. Or were they?

A standard military-issue M16 assault rifle has a seven-pound pull on the trigger. When the shooter squeezes the curved metal flange, it makes a clicking noise right before the firing pin connects with the primer on the first round. It is only a fraction of a second between trigger pull and round ignition—but you can hear it.

"Ambush right! Ambush right!" someone screamed.

From the high brush to my right, the sound of blank fire erupted in a deafening roar. The ambush was on.

Simultaneously, all the men in the platoon dropped to the ground and returned fire into the tall grass.

"Grenade! Grenade!" another voice shouted out.

To my immediate left, just to the side of the point man, a grenade simulator exploded, first one, then another, booming in my ears with stunning effect. On the ground around me, my platoon continued to fire, changing magazines and waiting for me to give the order to move. We couldn't counterattack through the brush; it was too thick. We couldn't move to the right; the instructors had sealed off our exit. It appeared that our only choice was to move left and try to get out of the kill zone. In my mind I knew that was the textbook answer, *but I had a better idea.*

Without hesitation, I jacked another magazine into my M16, jumped up from my prone position, and ran around the left edge of the heavy brush, nodding to the point man as I bolted past him. I would flank the instructors, circle around the bushes, come up from behind them, and counter-ambush them myself. *This was going to be awesome.*

Like a man possessed, I charged past the row of bushes, jumped over a few small boulders, and found myself unopposed on the high ground behind the instructors. Flipping my selector switch to full auto, I pulled the trigger and raked the bodies of the seven men lying behind the high brush. I moved forward, continuing to fire as I methodically shot each man with blank ammunition.

We had won!

"What the hell are you doing, Mr. Mac?" Instructor Faketty yelled, jumping up from the ground.

"Killing bad guys," was my quick and proud retort.

Doc Jennings, one of the few Black frogmen of the Vietnam era, stood up from where he was lying and gave me a look of complete disdain.

"Sir, you're a damn fool," he said, or words to that effect.

"You left your platoon lying in the kill zone. Did they know what you were doing?"

Somehow, this wasn't going as I had imagined.

"Get back with your platoon, Mr. Mac," Jennings said sternly.

I thought the worst of my ass-chewing was over. Surely the platoon would appreciate my quick thinking. They would understand what I was trying to do. I had defeated the instructors. That must count for something.

"Sir, what the hell were you thinking?" Varner said, echoing the words of Faketty.

"We had no idea where you went," LeBlanc piped in.

I quickly tried to explain.

"Look, guys. I saw an opportunity to flank the enemy and save the platoon. I reacted."

"Well sir, that's just fine, but we had no clue what you were doing or where you were going."

Marshall Lubin had swung around to join in the conversation.

"Yeah, man. I thought you were running away from the firefight."

"No, no, no! Come on, guys. I was trying to save the platoon."

"Sir, with all due respect," Varner said, a little less caustic now, "your job was to get us out of the kill zone, to communicate your intent so we could all move together and survive."

I just nodded. I knew they were right.

Jim Varner's words stayed with me for the rest of my career. *Your job was to get us out of the kill zone, to communicate your intent so we could all move together and survive.*

There is nothing more daunting, no greater crisis, than being caught in a real ambush, with real bullets and real lives on the line. But whether you are experiencing an existential threat or just a challenging time in your business, a successful leader knows that you must communicate your actions to the rank and file. If you want everyone in the organization to move as one, you must ensure that even the lowest-level employee understands your intent and follows your directions.

On the first page of the *U.S. Army Ranger Handbook* are the standing orders for "Rogers' Rangers." The Rangers were organized in 1756 by Major Robert Rogers. He recruited nine companies of American colonists and trained them to fight in the French and Indian War. Rogers was an accomplished hunter, tracker, and soldier from New Hampshire. He put down in writing nineteen "standing orders" that all his Rangers had to memorize. Although these rules are over two hundred years old, every modern-day Army Ranger has them memorized. For over two centuries, these rules were reinforced every day by the chain of command. They were communicated first by posting them on a tree, then in the written text of the *Ranger Handbook*, and now on the internet—everyone who wears a Ranger Tab understands what they must do in the field.

During my time commanding a joint special operations unit, we had troops stationed all around the world. In one day we would sometimes conduct six video tele-conferences, constantly ensuring the leaders in the field understood my orders, while at the same time getting feedback from the lowest-ranking soldier.

A few years later, when I commanded all of U.S. special operations, we routinely conducted all-hands meetings, had live broadcast town halls, and disseminated an assortment of written correspondence. Additionally, I directed that my "Commander's Intent," the values and goals of the organization, be displayed in every office and on every desk. After retiring from the military, I took the same philosophy of overcommunicating to the University of Texas System.

Everyone understands the importance of good communications, but time and time again, leaders fail to ensure that their goals, objectives, values, and intentions are clearly understood by the rank and file. Communications require constant effort on the part of the leader. It is not something you can leave solely to a staff member. You have to be intimately involved to ensure that the message is clearly delivered and that you are receiving the feedback necessary to make organizational changes where required.

Sooner or later, every leader gets ambushed with trouble. Maybe it's a crisis, maybe it's a kerfuffle, maybe it's just a misunderstanding, or maybe it's an opportunity. Just remember, if you're going to move out aggressively, make sure everyone knows what you're doing: communicate, communicate, communicate.

It's Simple:

1. Establish a means for communications to flow in both directions.
2. Confirm that the values and the goals of the organization are understood down to the lowest-ranking member.
3. Never take a significant action without having a plan for informing the rank and file.

CHAPTER SIXTEEN

When in Doubt, Overload

Nothing ever comes to one,
that is worth having, except
as a result of hard work.

—BOOKER T.
WASHINGTON

The storm front was moving quickly, the dark clouds rising high above the horizon and the winds gusting to twenty knots. The chop on the water off San Clemente Island was making it difficult to locate the concrete obstacles lodged in the sand ten feet below.

Through the fog and seawater in my mask, I spotted another scully—a large four-by-four-foot concrete block with protruding steel beams—half buried by the surging tide. Grabbing my satchel charge, I free dived down to the steel beams embedded in the obstacle and placed the explosives flush against the concrete. The obstacle was huge and right in the path of the amphibious landing. If it wasn't destroyed, the Mike boats carrying the Marines would have to divert and the landing would be aborted.

As a new ensign in Underwater Demolition Team Eleven, I had been put in charge of a small team of twenty-one frogmen. The Navy and Marine exercise controllers had strewn ten scullies in the path of the amphibious assault force. Our job was to clear the obstacles for the beach landing. While it was only an exercise, the potential for serious injury was high. If a Mike boat got hung up on the steel beams and couldn't maneuver out of the surf, the possibility of capsizing was real.

Prior to the exercise, we had conducted detailed planning to ensure we had the right amount of plastic explosives, the correct yardage of detonation cord, the exact number of time fuses and blasting caps, and then as always, sufficient spares. Since WWII, Navy frogmen had been clearing beaches across the Pacific and in preparation for the landing at Normandy. Interestingly enough, the basics of clearing the beach haven't changed since then. A team of frogmen would board a high-speed craft. The boat would approach the beach and drop off the frogmen parallel to the shoreline in water about twenty-one feet deep. Using a plastic slate, a grease pencil, and a lead line, the frogmen would swim the distance in to the beach, diving down along the way to locate the obstacles.

Once each man made his way to the beach and back, the high-speed boat would swing by and pick them up. Back on the mother ship, the leader would chart the location of the obstacles and plan the correct amount of explosives necessary to destroy them. These calculations were precise. For each scully, a haversack of twenty pounds of C-4 was necessary. Once all the explosives were assembled, the frogmen would reboard the high-speed craft, head back to the beach, load the obstacles with explosives, and detonate the C-4, clearing the way for the Marines. But forty years of clearing beaches from Okinawa to Normandy to Inchon to Vietnam had taught the frogmen one very important lesson: Whenever you were in doubt about the amount of explosives to use— *always overload*. Always put more energy, more force, more power into the solution than seemed necessary. It was the only way to guarantee success in the face of uncertainty and doubt.

Five years later, I was assigned to an East Coast SEAL Team and I was fired, relieved of my command, and re-assigned to another Team. At the time it seemed like my career was over. It's never good to get fired, but it's really bad to be fired in the Navy and particularly bad to be fired in the SEAL Teams, because everybody knows who you are.

Fortunately, Commander John Sandoz and Lieutenant Commander Jon Wright, both of whom I had worked for at UDT-11, believed in me and gave me another chance at a new SEAL Team. I knew that second chances were few and far between, and the only way I was going to earn back the respect of my fellow frogmen was to work harder—work harder than anyone believed necessary, work harder than the calculations called for, work harder than the obstacles in my path. If there was any doubt about my commitment, my competence, my professionalism, I would overload my effort into everything required to succeed. Every day the refrain *When in Doubt, Overload* echoed in my head. I would leave nothing to chance when it came to my determination. In the next year, I would complete a successful SEAL deployment, earn back the respect of my fellow SEALs, and reinvigorate my career.

Twenty-five years later, however, I would find myself in a similar situation. Having been promoted to vice admiral and just taken charge of a special operations command, I saw an opportunity to capture several key figures in the al Qaeda network we were pursuing. The only problem was—the al Qaeda fighters were hiding in a country where on-the-ground operations were off-limits owing to the political sensitivity. However, after months of making my case to the CIA, the Pentagon, the State Department, and the White House, I received approval for the mission. I was warned by several colleagues that if this went poorly, my time in command could be cut short. Despite this, I thought the intelligence gained from capturing these men would be well worth the risk.

Unfortunately, instead of capturing the five bad guys, the SEALs on the mission got into a fierce firefight with the enemy, and the mission had to be aborted. While everyone got back safely, it was clear that my plan and my leadership of the operation had failed. In the days that followed, I received a lot of scrutiny over the outcome, and at one point a senior officer was overheard to comment that "maybe McRaven is the wrong man for this job." Doubt had seeped into the psyche of my superiors—doubt about my competence, doubt about my leadership—and quickly that doubt began to spread. I have to admit, even I had doubts about myself. But experience had taught me that the only way to resolve those doubts was to put more effort into the job—*time to overload*.

I got up earlier, worked longer, went out on more tactical operations, studied the battlefield incessantly, and slept a lot less, and then, when the next opportunity presented itself, I was ready. Hard work creates opportunities. It's that simple. And if you have stumbled along the way, then doubling your efforts invariably exposes new opportunities to succeed. Every leader fails occasionally, and those failures can create doubts about your vision, your plan, your commitment, your talent, and your leadership. Always remember: When in Doubt, Overload.

It's Simple:

1. Work hard. Everyone expects it from their leader.
2. Work harder. Give the extra effort. It will inspire the rank and file.
3. Work your hardest. It will open opportunities that didn't exist before.

CHAPTER SEVENTEEN

*Can You Stand Before
the Long Green Table?*

Ninety-nine percent of all failures come from people who have a habit of making excuses.

—GEORGE WASHINGTON CARVER

I n October of 1925, the nation was fixated on the court-martial trial of an American hero, General Billy Mitchell. Mitchell was a highly decorated pilot who had received the nation's second-highest award for valor for his exploits in aerial combat during WWI. But Mitchell was also a fierce advocate for air power, believing that another war was on the horizon and that a unified air force should be built to rival the Army and the Navy.

Mitchell was particularly adamant that airplanes carrying heavy bombs could sink a battleship. However, the Navy leadership and the White House had made a case to Congress for additional battleships and defended their position vehemently. To prove their point, the Navy orchestrated several demonstrations of the battleships' survivability, but the exercises were rigged in the Navy's favor and Mitchell exposed the deception. Finally, after insisting on a legitimate test, Mitchell proved beyond a doubt that air power could dominate at sea and on land. Nevertheless, the services fought back hard against the idea of a unified air force. Mitchell was eventually court-martialed when he accused the Army and Navy leadership of "almost treasonable administration of the national defense."

The court-martial had a jury of thirteen military officers, including a young major general named Douglas Mac-Arthur. Among those who testified on Mitchell's behalf were a Who's Who of military royalty, including WWI ace Eddie Rickenbacker, General Hap Arnold, and General Carl Spaatz. The latter two officers would go on to lead the U.S. Air Force.

Over the course of the seven-week trial, Mitchell stood before the "long green table" of assembled officers and made his case. He never wavered from his position that he had a moral, legal, and ethical obligation to raise these issues to the leadership of the Army and the Navy. War was coming, he stated, and a failure to recognize the inevitable and plan for the fight was near treasonous.

In spite of all the support he received, and his passionate defense, Mitchell was found guilty on all counts. Of the thirteen-member jury, MacArthur was the only officer who voted to acquit. He said, "A senior officer should not be silenced for being at variance with his superiors in rank and accepted doctrine."

Seven years later, one of Mitchell's early critics, Franklin

Delano Roosevelt, became his strongest advocate. By 1942, the skies over Germany were filled with American bombers, and in 1947, by an act of Congress, the United States Air Force was established. History would reflect that Billy Mitchell stood tall in the face of withering criticism and career-ending threats. For his unwavering support of air power and his principled stand on aviation mobilization, General Billy Mitchell would forever be known as the Father of the Air Force.

Difficult decisions with serious ramifications require careful thought. Throughout my career I often found myself on the horns of a dilemma, torn between what I knew to be right and what others expected or what was expedient. At these times I always came back to the question, *"Can you stand before the long green table?"* Can you justify to reasonable men and women, sitting in judgment of your decisions, that the actions you are taking are moral, legal, and ethical and conform to the goals and objectives of the organization? If not, you should reconsider your actions. But if you can honestly say that your actions are justified, that reasonable people would see them as such, then stand by your convictions and make the hard choices.

———

In 2001, Enron Corporation, an energy and commodities firm located in Houston, was found to be systematically and willfully defrauding its customers. The fallout resulted in prison sentences for the company leaders, the dissolution of Enron, and the downfall of one of the top accounting firms in the world. In their insightful book *The Smartest Guys in the Room: The Amazing Rise and Scandalous Fall of Enron*, Bethany McLean and Peter Elkind point out that a number of senior employees within the organization knew that something was wrong, but the company was making millions, so they let it slide. These executives rationalized their actions in several ways and never confronted the obvious corruption. In the epilogue of *Smartest Guys*, the authors note that "The after-the-fact rationalizations [by the accused executives] were strikingly similar to the mind-set that brought about the Enron disaster in the first place. The arguments were narrow and rules-based, legalistic in the hairsplitting sense of the word." In other words, the leaders were trying to find a way to rationalize bad behavior because they were making so much money.

The same can be said for a number of universities that stretched athlete recruiting rules, turned a blind eye toward sexual misconduct, or allowed big donors special privileges. They convinced themselves that winning a national championship, a Nobel Prize, or a large gift would bring the students more resources, and therefore their actions were justifiable.

Sooner or later the actions of every leader will be scrutinized both externally and internally. To avoid the missteps that ruin so many careers and institutions, there are three questions that should be applied to every decision and every action: *Is it ethical, legal, and moral?*

Ethical—does it follow the rules?

Legal—does it follow the law?

And moral—does it follow what you know to be right?

While most folks might think that knowing what is morally right or wrong can sometimes be ambiguous, *it is not*. In talking to both subordinates and superiors who made a bad decision and had to live with the consequences, invariably they said, "In the back of my mind I knew it wasn't right, but..." But they found a way to justify it.

I have found in my years of leading that when confronted with a challenging decision, I almost always know the right answer. It's just that the right answer is hard to accept, and the decisions are hard to make, because we do not live in a world of isolation. Making a hard decision will sometimes lose you friends. People will be mad at you. Short-term gains may be lost. You may even be court-martialed. But if you understand that sooner or later you will have to account for your actions, then by deciding to do what is moral, legal, and ethical, you will most likely end up on the right side of history.

It's Simple:

1. Ensure that all your decisions are moral, legal, and ethical.
2. Ask yourself if reasonable people would accept what you are doing as good and decent.
3. Sooner or later, you will be held to account for your actions. Always do the right thing.

CHAPTER EIGHTEEN

Always Have a Swim Buddy

---- ✶ ----

Lots of people want to
ride with you in the limo,
but what you want is
someone who will take the
bus with you when the
limo breaks down.

—OPRAH WINFREY

The greatest compliment one frogman can bestow on another is to call him "a swim buddy." It's a simple term, but it conveys everything about how we live, how we fight, and sometimes how we die.

Underwater at night when it is the darkest, it is your swim buddy who swims beside you—always ready to provide you air if you run out, untangle your lines if you're caught under a ship, or fend off unwanted visitors.

When parachuting, it is your swim buddy who checks your parachute before you jump, who ensures you pull at the right altitude. And it is your swim buddy who lands beside you in enemy territory.

When patrolling in combat, it is your swim buddy who walks on your flank—covering your six. It is your swim buddy who lays down a base of fire so you can maneuver against the enemy. And sometimes, it is your swim buddy who lays down their life for yours.

You learned it early in SEAL training, that you never did anything, at any time, without a swim buddy, someone who could bail you out of a tough situation. Your swim buddy was more than a diving partner, your swim buddy was your protection, your conscience, your friend, and frequently your salvation.

———

I turned off the video teleconference and sat in stunned silence. The doctors from Fort Bragg had just called my headquarters in Bagram, Afghanistan, to notify me that the results of my bone biopsy had just come back.

I had cancer.

The three doctors on the video assured me that the cancer was treatable, "the best kind to get if you're going to get cancer," but it was likely going to put an end to my SEAL career.

After taking several deep breaths to compose myself, I walked out of the small room and back to my office down the hall. Waiting for me was my irrepressible command sergeant major, Chris Faris. Faris had been with me for three years at that point. He was my right-hand man. The thing about war is that it complicates all decisions. As a leader, you sometimes struggle with doing what is right for the mission, right for the troops, and right for your moral compass. Faris always ensured that my three priorities were well aligned.

"Admiral, my Admiral! How are you today, sir?" Faris smiled as I walked in the door.

"Fine," I said, having difficulty focusing.

"You alright?" Faris asked.

I looked up from the ground.

"Yeah, fine."

Faris glanced over at my executive officer, Lieutenant Colonel Art Sellers, who was sitting at a plywood desk in the center of the room. He looked concerned. Sellers and Faris had a great relationship. They could seemingly communicate telepathically.

"Okay, boss. What's up?" Faris asked.

I walked into my inner office and Faris followed.

"I just got off the VTC with the docs from Fort Bragg."

"And..." Faris said somewhat hesitantly.

"And... they told me I have cancer."

Faris went quiet.

"How bad?"

"They say it's manageable, but they tell me I have to get back to Bragg immediately and start treatment."

Faris took a seat. I could tell he was debating how to handle the news. Do you commiserate? Pity? Give hope?

"Hey, don't sweat it, boss. You'll get through this."

Faris looked up at the clock. It was almost time for my morning operations and intelligence briefing, a brief involving the entire worldwide command.

"You need to get ready for the O&I. Come on."

I wasn't ready for anything. But Faris insisted.

Stepping directly in front of my desk, he looked me square in the face and said, "We still have a mission to do, and folks are counting on you."

It's not what I wanted to hear. I wanted the sergeant major to be sympathetic. I wanted the world to know that I was hurting, that I needed their support. I wanted someone to feel sorry for me.

"Sir," Faris said sternly. "Let's go."

Reluctantly, I got up out of the chair and walked down the long hall toward the larger command center.

As I entered the room, everyone stood. I took my seat at the center of the table. I was struggling. They were all looking at me for some initial words. Before I could speak, Faris asked for last night's casualty report. Who had been injured? Any killed?

As the report of several wounded was broadcast across the net, Faris gave me that look. I had seen it a hundred times before. It was the look that said, *Are you listening, Admiral?*

I listened.

I understood.

How did my minor diagnosis compare to the young men and women who had been shot or struck by an IED? What did I have to whine about?

I was in charge. *Do your damn job!*

Faris asked about a few of the injured and then turned the microphone over to me.

A small, knowing grin came over his face. He had done exactly what I needed him to do.

Now it was time for me to step up.

In the years that Chris Faris and I had been together, we had gone on dozens of combat missions, been involved in highly sensitive and successful operations to rescue hostages, raid compounds, and conduct missile strikes. Not all missions had gone well, and they frequently took their toll on my morale. At times, the burden of command was overwhelming, and had it not been for Faris's unwavering support, his ability to read my thoughts, to know when to speak, when to console, when to chastise, when to joke, when to harass, and when to follow, I would not have commanded as well.

After my diagnosis, Chris Faris kept me focused on what was important. He commiserated when it was right to do so, but he never let me feel sorry for myself. *It was tough love.* The kind of love you need when you think you're the only person in the world with problems. The kind of kick in the butt that a good swim buddy never hesitates to give, because he or she is there for you. In that year, I managed to get my cancer in check, my career stayed on track, and with Chris Faris by my side, we conducted the mission that got Osama bin Laden.

———

I have seen many an organization where the president or CEO believe that they must be strong enough, by themselves, to withstand the daily pressure of leadership. They believe that showing any sign of weakness, to anyone in the organization, will undermine their position. While I have often said that a leader "is not allowed to have a bad day," that pertains only to their demeanor in public. In public, before the rank and file, before the employees or the stockholders, a leader must never whine, never look defeated or dejected. If they do, their sullen attitude will spread like wildfire throughout the organization. However, every leader does have bad days. Every leader does need someone to talk to. Every leader must find someone they can trust.

Swim buddies are a necessity in life. Call them wingmen, copilots, first mates, shotgun riders, Skipper and Gilligan, Thelma and Louise, Barney and Fred, brothers, sisters, husbands, wives, partners—call them whatever you like, but without a good swim buddy you will be destined to make bad decisions, you will be confronted with the difficulties of life alone, you will sometimes wallow in self-pity, and nothing you do will be as fulfilling.

Every frogman knows that in the turbulent waters of life you always need a good swim buddy.

It's Simple:

1. Find a person you can trust implicitly. Be prepared to lean on them in times of great stress.
2. Accept both their support and criticism with equal grace.
3. Be a swim buddy to others. Someone out there needs you!

CONCLUSION

I n his best-selling novel *Gates of Fire*, Steven Pressfield tells the story of the Battle of Thermopylae in 480 BC. The Persian army of one hundred and fifty thousand men, under the command of Xerxes the Great, was marching on Greece—and the only thing that stood between Xerxes and the destruction of the Western world were three hundred Spartans led by King Leonidas.

The Spartans secured the narrow pass at Thermopylae and under the leadership of Leonidas held out against the Persians for three days before they were all slaughtered except for one man. But the toll on the Persian army was so great that eventually Xerxes retreated, never to return.

As the Persians were leaving Greece, Xerxes had the surviving Spartan brought before him. Severely wounded and exhausted from the fight, the Spartan stood defiantly before Xerxes. Xerxes wanted to know why the three hundred Spartans had fought so hard. Why had they sacrificed everything for this King Leonidas? What was it about the king that made him such a great leader?

And the Spartan replied.

"A king does not abide within his tent while his men bleed and die upon the field. A king does not dine while his men go hungry, nor sleep when they stand at watch upon the wall. A king does not command his men's loyalty through fear nor purchase it with gold; he earns their love by the sweat of his own back and the pains he endures for their sake. That which comprises the harshest burden, a king lifts first and sets down last. A king does not require service of those he leads but provides it to them…"

While *Gates of Fire* is a fictionalized account of the battle, there is no finer description of leadership than the final words of Pressfield's last Spartan. But few of us are King Leonidas, and most of our leadership challenges will not rise to the level of saving the Western world. However, whether you are holding off an invading army or just leading a small team at a coffee shop, the principles of leadership still apply.

First and foremost, you must strive to be a leader with integrity; be honest, be fair, don't lie, cheat, or steal. Find a moral code that speaks to you: the West Point Honor Code, the Girl Scout Law, the Hippocratic Oath, or scripture from the Christian Bible, the Quran, or the Hebrew Bible. Embrace ethical behavior and know that even when you stumble, you can find your way back to a life of honor. Also understand that by being a leader with integrity, you are creating a strong culture for your organization, because the culture of every organization begins at the top. If you don't live up to the standards of good conduct, how can you expect others to do so?

While being a person of character is the foundation of leadership, it alone is not sufficient for success. You must be competent as well. When you have both good character and competence, then you gain the trust of your bosses, your colleagues, and your subordinates. With trust, people will follow you. Without trust, you may find yourself charging the hill alone or guarding the pass alone.

As a leader you must have a little swagger, a healthy confidence that you are the right person for the job. Your self-assurance will instill confidence in others, confidence that they can meet the challenges, confidence that no matter the obstacles, you will rise to the occasion and lead them to success. But don't mistake cockiness for confidence. You must be humble enough to see the value in every member of the team, and humble enough to seek counsel when needed. It is not mutually exclusive to be both confident and humble.

Being a leader is exhausting at times. Imagine the

doctors and nurses on the front line of COVID, or the first responders at the Twin Towers, or the young Army captains in Ramadi, or members of the Female Engagement Teams in Afghanistan. The days are long, the stakes are high, the pressure is sometimes unbearable. It seems like every organizational burden rests on your shoulders. That is why being a leader requires such stamina. You must be physically, emotionally, and spiritually strong. Your employees will feed off your strength, but if you show fatigue and tiredness, and if you are dragging from the challenges, it will drain the energy from your employees, and the organization will suffer.

Problems are at the heart of leadership: a ragtag army fighting the British, a union of states dissolving, the Japanese Imperial fleet on your doorstep, exploding oil rigs, supply chain disruption, parents unhappy about school, a Little League team that can't scrap out a win. If you're not prepared to tackle the hard problems, then you are not leadership material. And the only way to address a tough challenge—is head-on. Don't equivocate, don't sidestep the issue, don't defer it to someone of lesser rank; take the initiative. Show your leadership and jump in with both feet.

In our hearts, we all love a gambler: the coach who calls

a trick play, the financier who bets on a penny stock, or the general who plans a daring raid. We love it when the odds are against us and we come out on top. We want our leaders to be risk-takers because everyone understands that "nothing ventured, nothing gained." But always remember, there is a difference between taking risks and being too cavalier. As a leader you can't be careless with the well-being of your employees, your company's resources, or the future of the organization. Be a risk-taker, but manage that risk through extensive planning, preparation, and proper execution.

Those who succeed as leaders have personal qualities that set them above the commonplace. They are honorable and trustworthy, confident yet humble, they have stamina, initiative, and aren't afraid to take risks. These qualities are the foundation of good leadership, but good leaders must also take actions to achieve their goals.

Father John Jenkins, the president of Notre Dame, once said, "Let no one ever say we dreamed too small." The great leaders of this world never dream too small. They have a bold vision—a man on the moon, eradicating smallpox, equality for all, building a world on sustainable energy, a high school team going to the championship, or a new business model. And in addition to that vision, leaders must have a firm foundation in detailed planning and hard work (not just wishful thinking).

An important corollary to having that plan is understanding that no plan is ever executed perfectly. Chance and uncertainty invariably come into play. Whether your plan is a grand strategic undertaking or a small tactical engagement, always be prepared to adjust the plan to the circumstances before you. Have a Plan B. And often a Plan C, D, and E.

Every vision, every corporate strategy, every grand plan must identify benchmarks set by the leader to drive the organization to excellence. The rank and file want to be challenged. They want to be on an exceptional team with high standards, lofty expectations, and stretch goals. Everyone wants to be a winner.

Every great leader I served with understood the need to share the hardships with the men and women they led. Nothing gains the respect of the troops quicker than spending time on the factory floor, or in the trading room, the warehouse, the clinic, or the foxhole.

The C-suite, the corner office, the front office, or the largest cubicle can trap you into believing that your place is above the people you serve. It is not. Wherever you sit as a leader, don't sit for long. Get out of your office and spend time with the employees. This will give you an appreciation for the work they do, an understanding of the challenges they face, and insights into how to improve the business.

Your job as a leader is to ensure the organization is running as efficiently and as effectively as possible. This means continuous and appropriate oversight. The rank and file will resist, but if they know that this is your priority and that you participate in the inspections and are inspected yourself, then they will accept it as an important and worthwhile undertaking for the institution.

Through all of these steps, communicating clearly serves to synchronize the workforce from top to bottom. So, whether you are setting the vision, building the strategy, developing the plan, or inspecting the factory, always ensure you are communicating your goals, your expectations, and most importantly, your appreciation. The employees may or may not like the direction you have set for the organization, but they will always be grateful for knowing what you are thinking and where you are headed as a leader.

Jefferson was quoted as saying "the harder I work, the more luck I seem to have." I would offer that nothing in your leadership tool kit is as valuable as hard work.

Hard work creates opportunities. Hard work endears you to your workforce. Hard work increases your knowledge, your understanding, your empathy, and your insights. Hard work will overcome your shortfalls in talent. And when you stumble as a leader, nothing repairs the damage as quickly as hard work.

By definition, every leader is responsible for something. If you are responsible for the coffee shop, the burger joint, the retail store, the elementary school, the high school, the university, the corporate office, the hospital, the Wall Street bank, or the government agency, then you are also accountable: accountable to your workers, your customers, your employers, and your regulators. The buck stops with you. Great leaders accept the responsibility and the accountability. Always ensure your actions and decisions are moral, legal, and ethical.

Finally, no leader is immune from the pressures of the job. To be successful, we all need a strong partner who can pick us up when we fall, dust us off, and give us encouragement to move forward, a partner who will tell us the truth, offer tough love, criticize without judgment, and guide us through the difficult times. Behind every great leader is a great partner.

———

In his book *It Worked for Me*, Colin Powell tells the story of the old general sitting in the officers' club who is approached by a brand-new Army second lieutenant. The general is on his third martini when the young lieutenant gets up the courage to approach the senior officer. The general is very courteous, and after some small talk, the lieutenant finally asks the question he's been dying to ask.

"How do you make general?" the lieutenant inquires.

"Well, son," the general answers, "here's what you do. You work like a dog, you never stop studying, you train your troops hard and take care of them. You are loyal to your commander and your soldiers. You do the best you can in every mission, and you love the Army. You are ready to die for the mission and your troops. That's all you have to do."

The lieutenant replies, "Wow, and that's how you make general?"

"Naw," replies the general. "That's how you make first lieutenant. Just keep repeating it and let them see what you've got."

Leadership is difficult, and after forty years of being in leadership positions, I am still learning how to be a better leader. I learn from my students in class, from my colleagues at work, from fellow board members, from my family and my friends. But like the advice from the old general, the one thing I know about leadership is that you must keep doing your best every single day and let them see what you've got. And always remember that while leadership is difficult, it's not complicated. I hope you will find the wisdom of this old bullfrog of some value on your road to being a better leader.

IT'S SIMPLE

DEATH BEFORE DISHONOR

(Be a person of integrity)

YOU CAN'T SURGE TRUST

(Be trustworthy)

WHEN IN COMMAND, COMMAND

(Be confident in yourself)

WE ALL HAVE OUR FROG FLOATS

(Have a little humility)

THE ONLY EASY DAY WAS YESTERDAY

(Demonstrate that you have stamina)

RUN TO THE SOUND OF THE GUNS

(Be aggressive in solving problems)

SUA SPONTE

(Encourage your employees to take the initiative)

WHO DARES WINS

(Be prepared to take risks)

HOPE IS NOT A STRATEGY

(Do the detailed planning necessary for success)

NO PLAN SURVIVES FIRST CONTACT WITH THE ENEMY

(Have a Plan B)

IT PAYS TO BE A WINNER

(Establish standards of conduct and performance)

A SHEPHERD SHOULD SMELL LIKE HIS SHEEP

(Spend time on the "factory floor")

TROOP THE LINE

(Listen to your employees)

EXPECT WHAT YOU INSPECT

(The quality of your work will depend on the quality of your oversight)

COMMUNICATE, COMMUNICATE, COMMUNICATE

(Communicate your actions)

WHEN IN DOUBT, OVERLOAD

(Work hard to overcome your shortfalls)

CAN YOU STAND BEFORE THE LONG GREEN TABLE?

(Be accountable for your actions)

ALWAYS HAVE A SWIM BUDDY

(Have a partner in your leadership journey)

For a printable version of the Wisdom of the Bullfrog, scan the QR code below.

ACKNOWLEDGMENTS

I wish to thank my friend Bob Barnett, who is always looking out for my best interests, and to my editor Sean Desmond and the great team at Hachette Books for their steadfast support.

ABOUT THE AUTHOR

Admiral William H. McRaven (U.S. Navy Retired) is the #1 *New York Times* bestselling author of *Make Your Bed* and the *New York Times* best-sellers *Sea Stories: My Life in Special Operations* and *The Hero Code: Lessons Learned from Lives Well Lived*. In his thirty-seven years as a Navy SEAL, he commanded at every level. As a Four-Star Admiral, his final assignment was as Commander of all U.S. Special Operations Forces. After retiring from the Navy, he served as the Chancellor of the University of Texas System from 2015 to 2018. He now lives in Austin, Texas, with his wife, Georgeann.